The Art of Personal Prayer

LANCE WEBB

Foreword by D. Elton Trueblood

Study Guide by Delia Halverson

Abingdon Press
Nashville

THE ART OF PERSONAL PRAYER

Copyright © 1962, 1977 Assigned to Abingdon Press

Published by Abingdon Press in 1992 as an Abingdon Classic
Previously published by The Upper Room and by Abingdon Press

Library of Congress Cataloging-in-Publication Data

WEBB, LANCE.
   The art of personal prayer/Lance Webb.
      p.   cm.—(Abingdon classics)
   Originally published: 1962.
   Includes bibliographical references.
   ISBN 0-687-0192-6 (pbk.: alk. paper)
   1. Prayer—Christianity. I. Title. II. Series.
BV215.W4   1992
248.3'2—dc20   92-9342

Scripture quotations, unless otherwise noted, are from the Revised
Standard Version of the Bible and are copyright 1946 and 1952 by
the Division of Christian Education of the National Council of
Churches of Christ in the U.S.A.

Scripture quotations from The New Testament in Modern English
translated by J. B. Phillips are copyright 1958 by J. B. Phillips and
are used by permission of The Macmillan Co.

Quotations from *He Sent Leanness: A Book of Prayers for the Natural
Man* by David Head are reprinted with permission of The
Macmillan Co. and The Epworth Press. Copyright © 1959 by the
Epworth Press.

MANUFACTURED IN THE UNITED STATES OF AMERICA

DEDICATED

to my spiritual guides, both ancient and modern,
through whose writings and personal influence
I have begun to discover and practice
some of the precious art of
Christian prayer

FOREWORD

Of the many books on prayer, this one written by Lance Webb is different. It is different because, in the effort to emphasize the power rather than the problem, it draws on a more extensive reservoir of resources than does the ordinary book on prayer. Instead of depending merely on his own unaided experience, Bishop Webb shares with the reader what he has learned from the spiritual insights of persons representing many centuries. Among those are Meister Eckhart, Brother Lawrence, Blaise Pascal, William Law, Rufus Jones, and Thomas Kelly. Other authors reveal some indebtedness, but few give evidence of such breadth.

The reader who wonders at the catholicity of Bishop Webb's approach to the subject learns, as he reads, how this has been possible. We are told how, fourteen years prior to the actual writing of this volume, the author devoted six weeks to the study of the lives of the saints. He did this, he says, because he had "found the hit-and-miss habits of prayer utterly inadequate." He realized that he needed to draw from wells deeper than his own. This is how he came to be familiar with the classics of devotion and to confront some of the best thinking devoted to the life of the spirit.

One tangible result of the experiment conducted thirty years ago was the decision to spend the first part of each working day, not in preparation for a sermon, "but in meeting God and learning to trust and listen."

The regularity of this interior discipline has become the chief secret of the author's effectiveness. It has been his secret weapon, but it is one which he now seeks to share with all who will listen.

Of all of the spiritual giants from whom Bishop Webb has learned, the one whom he resembles most is Rufus Jones. Like Professor Jones, Bishop Webb is drawn to the compelling idea that at the center of the spiritual life there is not a single search, but a double one. It is not merely that we seek God, but that God is always seeking us. If Rufus Jones had not already used the title *The Double Search*, this would have been a suitable title for the volume which is now reissued in paperback.

My hope is that the contemporary reissue of this undated book on the meaning of prayer will reach a new generation of readers who are hungry and who know that they are hungry. Without prayer, "there is a broken circuit in God's loving purposes," and any author who enrolls students in the school of prayer is performing an important service. I welcome this publication because Bishop Webb is one of the great teachers in this most important of schools. May there be many students!

D. ELTON TRUEBLOOD

CONTENTS

I. ADORATION

1. "I MUST FIRST NOT ASK BUT ADORE!"

Most of us begin our praying in the wrong place. We are like the little boy who, when asked by his pastor if he said his prayers every night, answered, "No, sir, not every night, some nights I don't want anything!"

Prayer at its best is meeting God in conscious, glad attentiveness; and who can meet the almighty, loving, all-wise Lord of the universe without what the saints have called adoration!

> In the castle of my soul
> Is a little postern gate
> Whereat, when I enter,
> I am in the presence of God.
> In a moment, in the turning of a thought,
> I am where God is,
> This is a fact.[1]
> —WALTER RAUSCHENBUSCH

If this is a fact—and countless of the greatest minds of all ages will stake their lives upon it—then it is the greatest fact known to our humanity!

Adoration is the beginning and ending of that com-

9

munion with the presence of God which indeed gives all life meaning, fulfills all my deepest desires, and brings me joy and strength and victory "in the great quiet of God."

One person described her experience in the words of the title of this section. Upset by troubles and distraught with conflicts and doubts, she got nowhere in her prayers. Her asking and seeking went unrewarded. Then she went into the sanctuary of her church. There in the quietness she opened the little postern gate of her soul and "in a moment, in the turning of a thought," she met God. She lost her feverish fretting "in wonder, love, and praise" as the old hymn says it. She forgot her problems for the moment as she lifted her heart in adoration before the wonders of his love and the greatness and might of his wisdom. When she came back once more to think of her problems, she saw them in a new light and received a new courage and strength to meet them. Thus it was she said, "I must first not ask but adore!"

One thing all great spirits in every religion agree upon: the adoration of God is the heart and soul of prayer. It does two things for us that nothing else can do: (a) it puts us and our problems in proper perspective so that all things begin to take on rightful proportions; and (b) it enables us to accept and receive the love and help of God and thereby enables us to love and serve others.

What the adoration of God is may be illustrated in the story of the little son of a busy preacher who pushed open the door of his dad's study, pulled a hassock close to his father's feet, and sat down with his round eyes fixed on his father's face. The father, who was behind in his sermon preparation, said rather impatiently to the little fellow, "Well, what is it? What do you want?" The big eyes grew wider in disappointment and the little fellow said reproachfully, "I don't want nuffin'. I'se only looking at you and lovin' you!" That moment the father understood better than ever before the meaning and power of adoration.[2]

Often we may come to God because of our dire needs, but before we have truly begun to pray we enter into a relationship of new appreciation of his greatness and goodness. Adoration is *looking* and *loving*. Asking may come later but when it comes, its spirit and results will be largely determined by the quality of our adoration. Evelyn Underhill says adoration is

the upward and outward look of joyful admiration, . . . awesome delight in the splendour and beauty of God . . . in and for himself alone, as the very color of life, giving its quality of unearthly beauty to the harshest, most disconcerting forms and the dreariest stretches of experience. This is adoration; not a difficult religious exercise, but an attitude of the soul.[3]

The most perfect prayer of all, which we call the Lord's Prayer, begins with adoration:

> Our Father who art in heaven,
> Hallowed be thy name.

To hallow the name of God is to recognize and rejoice in his majesty, his greatness, his everlasting love. It is not merely thinking about God, but in his presence looking and loving.

What, then, should we seek first in our prayers? Not visions and voices. Not feelings of any kind or great emotional experiences. Not what we call "blessings," "consolations," or even help with our direst problems. But first we should seek to meet and adore God in loving attentiveness. For in this divine stillness God gives us his peace and quiets our storms. He drops the "still dews of quietness, till all our strivings cease." He takes "from our souls the strain and stress" until "our ordered lives confess the beauty of [his] peace." And often we find a solution to our pressing problems. Indeed! But we seek not first of all peace but God. Our need for peace may bring us prayer, but we do not find peace except as first and primarily we seek God. When we look and love and adore, peace will come, as will the answer to our deepest needs, but only when we want God and wait in glad attention before the glory and grandeur of his presence.

Then:

> All life has a meaning,
> Without asking I know:
> My desires are even now fulfilled,
> My fever is gone
> In the great quiet of God.
> My troubles are but pebbles on the road,
> My joys are like the everlasting hills.[4]

So may you—even as you read—open up the "little

postern gate" in your mind, enter, and be thankful in the joyful adoration of God! No experience can be more productive of creative power for worthy living. No experience is more distinctively human in the sense that it is for this that we are made and in this our lives are at their best.

2. "BIG THINGS BECOME SMALL, AND SMALL THINGS BECOME GREAT."

Adoration puts us and our problems in the proper perspective so that we and they begin to take on rightful shape and importance.

When my little, hurried, tense, bothered soul is quieted in the presence of the steadfast love of God who never hurries, never frets, never fails—when at last I am conscious of his greatness and grandeur, the majesty of his love:

> My fever is gone
> In the great quiet of God.
>
> .   .   .   .
>
> So it is when my soul steps thru the
>   postern gate
> Into the presence of God.
> Big things become small, and small
>   things become great.[5]

These hopeful words are not some farfetched ideal but rather the description of the experience of one of the most practical and Christlike men who ever lived, Walter Rauschenbusch. He is called "The Prophet of the Social Awakening," because in the period of greatest industrial expansion in American history, when persons were being enslaved to things, he insisted on pouring out his life in the slums of a big city in a service of love to the little and disinherited. He had problems, opposition, persecution, weariness, discouragement, frustrations; and yet his life was one of creative, redemptive love. Truly in his life big things—as the world sees them—became small, and small things became great.

The adoration of God brings a true perspective to any life in any situation.

Now perspective is a word we use to describe the viewpoint from which we look at things. There are many perspectives—some totally false—some nearer the truth. Imagine the perspective of a flea in the wrinkle of an elephant's skin. Every time the elephant takes a mud bath, the flea must think it is a major catastrophe!

Our human perspectives have been widened exceedingly by science with its breathtaking vistas into the immensities of space and the equal vastnesses within the tiny atom. Sometimes, however, our view is so wide we lose all the meaning and value of things.

There are many different perspectives from which we human beings may look at life. In general these may be divided into two kinds.

First, the perspective of a black faith that sees our lives as insignificant flotsam and jetsam cast about on the ocean of infinitude with no meaning except what we in the moment choose to accept for ourselves. This is the perspective of the human flea on the epidermis of one of the meanest planets. It says that though man can do remarkable tricks with his mind and his hands he is still alone and orphaned without help in the midst of his terrifying responsibilities. The best he can do is to recognize the meaninglessness and, as Bertrand Russell says, "build as firmly as possible on the foundations of unyielding despair." [6] From such a viewpoint obviously there is no room for prayer. Then adoration of anything beyond ourselves is silly and therefore impossible.

The other viewpoint is the perspective of faith in the Living God, the Creator and Sustainer of all things, who is not only the Integrating Principle of Cosmic Force whose might is revealed in the unimaginable power and grandeur of millions of galaxies of billions of suns and planets in starry space. But he is also the Infinite Spirit who has come near to us in the lives of noble spirits in every age and supremely in Jesus Christ. Most precious of all the facts we may experience is the fact that there is a correspondence between our spirits and the Spirit of the Mighty God. Augustine expressed it like this: "Thou hast made us for Thyself and restless are our hearts until they rest in thee." God is not found primarily in the distant, the terrible, the awesome but also in the near and ordinary, in a baby born into a loving family in the little town of Bethlehem, and in our own hearts. "The Word became flesh and dwelt among us, full of grace and truth [reality]." (John 1:14.)

Without the perspective of the Incarnation—God revealed in our human flesh—we might tremble in awe before the mysteries of the universe, but we never adore that which merely terrifies and threatens. As Christians we believe that God has come into our human life revealing his love for us. At the same time he reveals the potential greatness that is in each of us waiting to be developed in the light of his love. With this perspective, there is room for adoration!

For to adore is to love and to praise with joyful gladness and thanksgiving. It is more than admiration or reverence before the mysteries of the universe. One might admire the thundering beauty of an atomic missile on its way to the potential murder of millions of persons; but one could not love it. One with a mathematical mind might be awed and mystified by the evidence that Einstein's relativity formula, $E=mc^2$, is verified in test after test; but one would never cry out in the darkness of despair with anything approaching adoration, "O X to the nth Power, make us one with Thee!" When we not only listen to the teaching of the Master Teacher but accept him as "the way, and the truth, and the life," we will cry in utter and overwhelming joy as we experience the nearness and love of God, "Our Father . . . , Hallowed be thy name. . . . For Thine is the kingdom, and the power, and the glory, for ever" (K.J.V.).

In the presence of God the Father of our Lord Jesus Christ there is warmth and light and love that makes all things, even the darkest moments of pain and sorrow, stand forth in new meaning. Life takes on dignity even in its worst moments.

This is the experience of countless persons in every age. "Through him," wrote the apostle Paul, "we have obtained access to this grace in which we stand, and we rejoice in our hope of sharing the glory of God. More than that, we rejoice in our sufferings, . . . because God's love has been poured into our hearts through the Holy Spirit which has been given to us." (Rom. 5:2-5.)

Jane Merchant, though an invalid since childhood, has become through the power of adoring prayer one of the most articulate and helpful of our American poets. The recipient of the 1953-55 prize of the National League of American Pen Women, she has brought as much courage and hope and joy to as many as any other living writer today. And yet she is the victim of a baffling bone disease that has left her a permanent invalid. Since she was twenty-three she has been deaf and she suffers from a chronic eye disorder. For years she has written lying flat on her back with her typewriter across her on a little table. And yet the secret of her courageous life is simple: Looking to God and loving him with adoring praise:

> Thou art not far from any one of us,
> However far we are, O Lord, from thee.
> Give us the grace of quietness to know
> Thy presence and thy holy harmony
>
> Within our hearts through all the hurried hours,
> Through all the clamorous din of busy days,
> Till in the listening silence of our souls
> There stirs a song of worship and of praise,
>
> A song of praise to thee for all thy love,
> A song of love for every living thing
> That thou, our Father and our God, hast made.
> O teach us to be still, that we may sing.[7]

Jean François Millet's famous painting, "The Angelus," says this truth more effectively than any words. It portrays a peasant farmer and his wife pausing in their work to listen with bowed heads as the bells announcing the Angelus ring out over the fields from the church tower in the village. As they wait in silence they look to God and love him. The strain and bitterness leave their souls, and their troubles as well as their work are seen in a new light.

We all need to have an Angelus time regularly in our lives, when through the adoration of God we can see life in a new perspective. Some period in every day when we can be still and know that he is God and love and adore him! Thus we may be prepared for action without feverish strain, rebellion, despondency, feelings of our own importance, or worries about our own success. Thus we may find a new dignity and tranquility, a truer perspective in which to work and play and sing and suffer and die! We are no longer tired and frustrated fleas, but sons or daughters of God with an eternal destiny!

In order to pray thus we do not need to build tall, philosophical descriptions of the Integrating Force Behind All Things, though the best thinking in this direction is helpful to any of us. A clearer grasp of the meaning of our faith in God should be sought, but we must not wait for full, intellectual understanding of all that God is. To do this would mean that no one of us, even the most learned, could ever pray. For the best words we may use in speaking of God are only symbols of his ineffable mystery and reality. He is infinitely greater than all our words about him.

Though the completeness of the majesty and glory, the beauty and love, the wisdom and power that is God is unsearchable beyond all human thought: yet the good news of our Christian faith declares that God has come near to us in the life of Jesus Christ. In the presence of the Holy Spirit of the Mighty Father whom we have seen revealed in Jesus Christ, the sunset and the mountain, the joy and the pain of human experience, the hopes and fears of all mankind are broken lights that lead us to glad adoration of him.

> Lord of all being, throned afar,
> Thy glory flames from sun and star;
> Center and soul of every sphere,
> Yet to each loving heart how near!
>
> Lord of all life, below, above,
> Whose light is truth, whose warmth is love,
> Before thy ever-blazing throne
> We ask no luster of our own.
>
> Grant us thy truth to make us free,
> And kindling hearts that burn for thee,
> Till all thy living altars claim
> One holy light, one heavenly flame.[8]
>
> —OLIVER WENDELL HOLMES

3. AN OPEN DOOR TO THE LOVING STRENGTH AND WISDOM OF GOD

From the adoration of God comes all the other priceless expressions of Christian prayer. Without it all prayer is futile and useless, less than Christian. Because of its lack many of our prayers get nowhere. When we adore and revere God with a thankful, loving spirit the door is always opened to the love and strength and wisdom of God. Hence all that will be said in the pages that follow concerning the other ways of praying will have adoration as its root and center.

We confess our sins. When we adore God we are able to confess our weaknesses and sins without the continued-unhealthy guilt and self-loathing that often accompanies such confession. For the nature and the name of the God and Father we adore is Love! Incarnate love is seen in the mercy and kindness of our Lord Jesus Christ whose righteousness and purity of life condemns our unrighteousness and impurity, but whose sacrificial love makes it possible for us to accept forgiveness and to forgive ourselves.

In the presence of God in Christ confession is natural, necessary, and healthy.

No man can look on God and live, live in his own faults, live in the shadow of the least self-deceit, live in harm toward His least creatures, whether man or bird or beast or creeping thing. The blinding purity of God in Christ, how captivating, how alluring, how compelling it is! The pure in heart shall see God! More, they who see God shall cry out to become pure in heart, even as He is pure, with all the energy of their souls.[9]

We commit our wills. No man can stay long in the presence of God in Christ without a loving commitment,

20

a dedication of all his powers to fulfill the purposes of his being. "Thy will be done" inevitably follows "Hallowed be thy name." For to recognize the love of God, to wait quietly before him is to see the ineffable glory of his truth, the grandeur of his purpose for us and all mankind, and to want it with all our hearts. We will always follow our deepest desire.

We petition him. No man can adore God and look on his loving truth without changing his desires. Adoration is the necessary prelude to petition that makes it right to pray for our needs; for only adoration will keep us from lifting up false needs. Then we can pray: Give us what we really need for our daily bread—physically, mentally, socially, spiritually. Lead us from the temptation to want the wrong things. Deliver us from the evil of the false and the unworthy.

We ask for forgiveness. No man can tarry long before the forgiving love of God as revealed in Christ, who "for our sake he made him to be sin who knew no sin," who "bore all my sins upon the tree," and still keep in his heart any root of bitterness or any vengeful feelings toward any other. Then we can pray: "Forgive us as we forgive each other."

We intercede for others. No man can bow in thankful adoration before the Presence of Eternal Love without bringing those whom he loves into that Presence. Prayer for others is as natural and as necessary as breathing once you stand amazed in the presence of the giving love of Christ. You cannot help but pray for others as you bring them into the circle of God's great love.

We live with greater trust. No man can look on God in Christ with adoration and not live with a serener trust, a more confident spirit, a new power to love, a new strength to suffer, new patience to bear, new hope to win, and new faith to dare!

4. "FOR THINE IS THE KINGDOM, AND THE POWER, AND THE GLORY, FOR EVER. AMEN."

Adoration not only puts my life in its true perspective, but enables me to receive the love and help of God. C. F. Andrews, the great Christian who had such tremendous influence on Mahatma Gandhi, tells us what learning to adore God meant to him:

Change came in my own prayer life after I had learnt more fully to take Christ at His word and to do what He commanded.

For when at last, in obedience to His precept, I began to put God first, in the quiet times of prayer when I was alone, instead of thinking of my own failures and my own needs, then a change began which gave me confidence and hope. . . . [I learned] I must meet God first . . . and must offer my love at His feet. . . .

It helped me, perhaps, most of all to remember that Christ Himself had offered in this manner His thanksgiving to His Heavenly Father and had received in His silent hours of prayer His power to heal and to bless. . . . Thus, little by little, my own wants and needs began to take an altogether secondary place in the daily prayer life. Instead of this, in the foreground there came into ever greater prominence the worship and the love of God.

22

He goes on to tell how he had been helped in his understanding of prayer by the story of Brother Bernard who once kept awake in order to hear how Francis of Assisi spent his time in prayer. To Brother Bernard's surprise the great saint kept repeating, " 'My God and my all'—'My God and my all,' " while tears of thankfulness and love showed the depths of his devotion. So this great Christian found that his prayers brought him hope and confidence to the extent that he gave himself in "praise and thanksgiving, mingled with the deepest awe of loving devotion," to what seemed to him best to correspond with the words 'Our Father in heaven, hallowed be Thy name.' " [10]

This is the order and spirit of all successful prayer. Put God first in your prayer. Give yourself to worship and love of God and you will begin to receive the courage and strength and hope you need.

As Peter Wust, the much loved professor of philosophy in Cologne, lay dying after a long illness, his pupils asked him to give them a parting message of counsel from the deepest experiences of his life. Here is what he said to them:

The magic key is not reflection, as you might expect from a philosopher, but it is prayer. Prayer as the most complete act of devotion makes us quiet, makes us objective. A man grows in true humanity in prayer. Prayer is the final humility of the spirit. The greatest things in existence will only be given to those who pray. In suffering one learns to pray best of all.[11]

The greatest things in human existence—love, courage, hope, peace, confidence—are given only to those who pray. And the prayer that opens the door to these gifts is the prayer of adoration, of complete devotion, that seeks not the gifts but the Giver.

I said to my soul, be still, and wait without hope
For hope would be hope for the wrong thing; wait without love
For love would be love of the wrong thing; there is yet faith
But the faith and the love and the hope are all in the waiting.
Wait without thought, for you are not ready for thought:
So the darkness shall be the light, and the stillness the dancing.[12]

—T. S. Eliot

"Our Heavenly Father, we adore thee, whose name is love, whose nature is compassion, whose presence is joy, whose word is truth, whose spirit is goodness, whose holiness is beauty, whose will is peace, whose service is perfect freedom, and in knowledge of whom standeth our eternal life."

II. CONFESSION

1. I MEET GOD AND ACCEPT THE REAL TRUTH ABOUT ME

O wad some power the giftie gie us
To see oursel's as ithers see us! [1]
—ROBERT BURNS

How much more priceless is the ability to see ourselves not only as others see us, but even as we really are. "What a man is in God's sight that he is, no more and no less." [2]

The prayer of adoration gives us a perspective of the true and the false in our lives. The prayer of confession makes it possible for us to accept the true while we deny and surrender the false. "You will know the truth, and the truth will make you free." There is no greater power for freedom to live the truth than the prayer of honest, sincere confession in the presence of God whom we meet in the living Christ.

For Christian prayer at its best is the focusing of one's attention through his conscious thoughts on God. When we enter by faith into his presence and recognize his amazing love that accepts us with all our failures and wrongs and inadequacies, and when our little souls are swept by the fires of adoration and thanksgiving, then it is we may enter into a completely new experience of illumination.

"Therefore, if anyone is *in Christ*, he is a new creation; the old has passed away, behold, the new has come. All this is from God, who through Christ reconciled us to himself and gave us the ministry of reconciliation." (II Cor. 5:17-18.) In this illumined moment which Paul calls being "in Christ" we begin to see ourselves as we are and not as our false, little self-image would paint us to be. And being reconciled to God we are reconciled to ourselves and to all others.

The prayer of confession when it is honest, clear-eyed, completely open to the truth is one of the most priceless experiences of human life, for it is the way by which I meet and accept reality. I admit all my weaknesses, my fears, my longings, my conflicts, to myself in God's presence. I see just how false most of my longings have been and how foolish are my conflicts. I recognize how often I have been like Don Quixote in my personal and social life, going out to fight the windmills I mistake for enemies with nothing except my own little sword. I begin to understand why my sword is broken and I am so crushed —all unnecessarily. And since no windmill, much less a real enemy, is ever conquered that way I renounce my folly and turn to a more creative way.

This is the nature of our human life. Each one of us has built around him the shell of a false universe made up of false desires and illusions. This shell in which we try to live must be destroyed. It is our worst enemy, for most of our worry, resentments, hates, jealousies, fears, and even physical pains and diseases are its results. The prayer of confession is the method by which we co-operate with God in ridding ourselves of this false exterior and opening the dark dungeons of our inner selves to the light of God's truth.

The real truth about you and me is infinitely better than the half-truths and falsehoods to which we cling. Why is it so hard to see the truth? Why do we build caves of illusion, shells of untruth? Psychologists can help us here part of the way.

I feel inferior, inadequate, afraid. Why? Psychologists tell us it may be because of what happened yesterday or the day or the years before. I was hurt, made to feel little, rejected. So now deep inside my unconscious mind I feel that I am little and insignificant. But I don't want to be. In fact I know that I am not really so little and insignificant (one reason for believing God has put his image deep inside of me); I know I am really worthy and important. So I seek to prove my worth to myself and the world. I brag and strut and do foolish things to get attention. Or else I crawl into my shell so as not to be hurt any more. I may seek to be rich and powerful, so no one can make me feel little or hurt me any more; but I am afraid I won't succeed. Or if I do succeed, I am always afraid I will lose my new exaltation and security. I am insecure, and my anxiety and worry boils up inside me causing any number of physical illnesses. The doctor tells me to stop worrying or I will kill myself. I cannot. Why? Because I am living in this false shell of false demands to be big and important. I cannot overcome my worry or my hate, so long as this is my deepest need.

The real truth about me is far more wonderful than this false ego I am trying to buttress and make secure. But here psychology stops short and only the prayer of faith can take me further. When I meet the loving wisdom and truth of God in prayer, I cease to blame and hurt those who hurt me. I refuse to run from the hurt or to escape within my shell. Instead I open my mind and heart to the truth. I ask God to dig me out of the holes of falsehood in which I have sought to escape and in which I have hidden my true self.

This kind of prayer has been productive in the lives of all great spirits in every age. David, after his foolish and hurtful love affair with Bathsheba which led him to cause her husband Uriah to be killed, stood one day before God in whose light he saw himself for what he was:

> Have mercy on me, O God,
>   according to thy steadfast love;
>   according to thy abundant mercy
>   blot out my transgressions.
>
> . . . .
>
> For I know my transgressions,
>   and my sin is ever before me.
>
> . . . .
>
> Create in me a clean heart, O God,
>   and put a new and right spirit
>   within me.
>
> —Ps. 51: 1, 3, 10

Another penitent spirit exclaimed, in wonder before the One from whose presence he could never hide:

> Search me, O God, and know my heart!
>   Try me and know my thoughts!
> And see if there be any wicked [foolish, false] way in me,
>   and lead me in the way everlasting!
>
> —Ps. 139:23-24

Young Isaiah, in the midst of discouragement and frustration, waited in the temple where he testified: "I saw the Lord sitting upon a throne, high and lifted up." After an exalting experience of adoration before the holiness and majesty of God, he too cried:

"Woe is me! For I am lost; for I am a man of unclean lips, and I dwell in the midst of people of unclean lips; for my eyes have seen the King, the Lord of Hosts!"

Then flew one of the seraphim to me, having in his hand a burning coal which he had taken with tongs from the altar. And he touched my mouth, and said: "Behold, this has touched your lips; your guilt is taken away, and your sin forgiven."

—Isa. 6:5-7

Even the ancient Kekchi Indians had an evening prayer which says: "Thou alone, O God, Thou who seest me, Thou who defendest me, along my journey in the darkness which is above me, and in every hindrance which Thou canst remove from me, O my God, O my Lord, of the mountains and of the valleys! I say that I think, but do Thou pardon, O Lord . . . my mistakes." [8]

Alfred Delp, a sincere German Christian, during a time of great trial before his execution by the Nazis on December 31, 1944, wrote:

The outcome of this time can be only a great inner desire for God and for his glorification. I must meet him in a new and personal way. I must beat down the walls that still stand between him and me. The tacit reservations must be completely cleared away. I must live the prayer of Nikolaus von der Flue,

"My Lord and God, take all from me that blocks my way to thee.

My Lord and God, give me all that speeds my way to thee.

My Lord and God, take this myself from me and give it as thine own to thee!" [4]

So all who have found the new life of the spirit testify: the old guilt and falseness has to be burned away as does the debris that clutters up our lives and shuts out the light. All the shells that block the way to the truth must go, and we see what these shells are and how to remove them only in the light of the Eternal Love who never lets us go!

Here we must look far beyond the help of psychology and psychiatry. These may be able to show us how we got into the mess we are in. But they cannot lead us to the light. Only the light of God in Christ can do that. As François Fénelon, French Christian of the seventeenth century, prayed he began to understand:

It is not I who have done this work, because it is not through self that we escape from self. . . . It is thou, Lord, who carrying thy light to the depths of my soul, impenetrable to all else, hast shown me all the ugliness there. I know well that by seeing it I have not changed it. . . . [Even the best psychological insight does not set one free.] I know well that my own eyes could not have discovered all my hideousness, but at least I see part of it, and I want to find it all. I see my self horrible, and I am at peace, because I want neither to flatter my vices, nor that my vices should discourage me. I see them now, and I bear this shame calmly. I am for thee against myself, O my God! Only thou couldst have divided me thus against my own self. Behold what thou hast done within me, and thou continuest to do it daily, to take away from me all the rest of the wicked [false, unworthy] Adam-life, and to complete the creation of the new man . . . which is renewed from day to day.[5]

Let us, after the fashion of all free spirits, continue our prayer, going from adoration to confession:

> Create in me a clean heart, O God,
>   and put a new and right spirit
>   within me.
>
> . . . .
>
> Prove me, O Lord, and try me;
>
> . . . .
>
> and lead me in the way everlasting!
> —Pss. 51:10; 26:2, 139:24

2. HONESTLY I FACE THE SIN AS WELL AS THE SYMPTOM

No human experience is more freeing and cleansing than sincere confession. "If we confess our sins, he is faithful and just, and will forgive our sins and cleanse us from all unrighteousness." (I John 1:9.) But not all confession has this result. The difficulty comes with being honest. "An honest confession is good for the soul," but how difficult it is to be honest with God and with ourselves! It is easy to use our conscience in criticizing others while at the same time we anesthetize it in behalf of our own exalted ego.

Now it is easy to confess the sins of others. And it is comparatively easy to confess the symptoms of our own sin: the alcoholic to confess that he ought to quit the alcohol that is destroying him, the thief to confess that he made a mistake when he is caught, or the ill-tempered man to confess that his bad temper is the cause of the trouble he is in. In the Old Testament story Achan, one of Joshua's soldiers, disobeyed the command not to loot the conquered city. He stole a bar of silver which he hid under the floor of his tent. When it was found, and only then, did Achan blurt out, "I have sinned."

So with us: "I'm sorry I lost my temper, Lord, and did such harsh things," I may say. But down deep in my heart I am saying, "I was really justified in being so ill-tempered and harsh; it was a mean thing he did to me." So I am not penitent at all for the things that made me lose my temper—the jabs at the little self-image I still hold sacred and before which I expect everyone to fall down and worship or at least recognize with approval!

Or I may say: "I'm sorry that I worry until I am weary and exhausted, Lord, and sick with fear; please help me to quit"; but deep down I am saying, "I am not at all sorry for the idol I have of what I want more than anything else and which I am unwilling to trust to God."

So often when we confess our sins, we stop with the symptoms—anxiety, worry, fear, ill-temper, hate—and the physical exhaustion resulting. We confess and repent that we are weak and afraid, but we never see or repent the root of self-will that makes us so.

It is never enough to pray, "God, give me peace of mind, help me control my temper, take away my hate!"

If this is as far as I go, my religion becomes an opiate, a means of escape. Suppose you do get rid of conscious hate and find some superficial peace? You may be worse off than before, for the resentments and fear still boil up inside and, finding no way out, may cause treacherous and devastating sickness and evils of body and mind. Many mental and physical ills are the result of covered up (repressed) hate and fear.

Kierkegaard had a story that applies to our present "peace-of-mind" cult. He tells the parable of a leper outside the city, longing to be well and to return to his family and friends. A traveling peddler offers to sell him a salve that will cover his sores so he can go into the city unnoticed. His problem is, "Shall I use the salve or not?" In a sense this is the problem our leprous souls also face continually as we are tempted by a superficial religion— a salve that may cover up and hide our real sins. Shall we cry, " 'peace, peace,' when there is no peace"? Shall we use our prayer as a salve? No. The apostle Paul said in effect that the only peace worthwhile is the fruit of the Spirit. The only love and joy and patience worth having are the by-products of having the Mind of Christ!

Oh, but this isn't easy, because I have my own mind, my self-image of life, my own way of thinking. "I would like to keep my own attitude toward life and have peace and joy and love too, if you please, Lord."

This is not possible according to Paul, "I die every day!" "It is no longer I who live, but Christ who lives in me." "Far be it from me to glory except in the cross of our Lord Jesus Christ, by which the world [of my false and inadequate self-image] has been crucified to me, and I to the world." (I Cor. 15:31; Gal. 2:20; 6:14.)

Pretty harsh words we think! Not at all considering the terrible fact of the sin which threatens me—the sin of self-centered anxiety causing me to close my eyes to the truth, seeking to remove the symptoms of my insecurity in my own way without doing anything to remove the cause, and wanting a small, finite good so that I am unable to see a higher good! This is the sin each of us must confess. Here is the one requirement for entering the Kingdom of Heavenly Life in Christ, as Jesus' words so clearly declare:

"If any man would come after me [to the freedom and joy and peace and love of the kingdom], let him deny himself [his self-idols] and take up his cross [the difficult things necessary to be free of his idols and to help others to be free] and follow me." (Mark 8:34.)

Honest confession goes beyond the symptoms to the roots of our sin. For in the words of the great Spanish Christian, St. John of the Cross, though outwardly I am

> Living, and [there is] no life in me?
> [I] languish in expectancy?—
> Dying to my dying day.
>
> Life within me? No, no spark.
> Without God is darkest dark!
> Failing him and failing me
> How can any life but be
> In extremis momently?
> Yearning for my life I say:
> Dying to my dying day!

. . . .

Seeing that what life I know
Has the face of death to show,
And that dying's all I do
Till I come alive in You! [6]

Such confession is costly, difficult, but the only way
we may truly come alive in him who brings us to true
life—"an everlasting day!"

Before we can confess our sin *honestly* we have to see
it. How does one discover these self-idols that keep us in
death, separated from God and life? Here are three suggestions taken from the lives of the saints:

First, sit or bow or kneel in the presence of the loving
wisdom and truth of God as seen in Jesus Christ or in
some great soul who has caught his spirit. Here wait,
worship, adore, and cry: "All goodness that is forever
and eternally good is in thee!" Or with Robert Browning
say: "There shall never be one lost good! What was, shall
live as before!" [7] Be confident that the truth of God's
love is infinitely more to be desired than any or all of
these false goals of mine. Therefore, O Lord:

I will delight in thy statutes;

. . ..

The law of the Lord is perfect,
reviving the soul;
the testimony of the Lord is sure,
making wise the simple;
the precepts of the Lord are right,
rejoicing the heart;
the commandment of the Lord is pure,
enlightening the eyes;

the fear of the Lord is clean,
    enduring for ever;

.   .   .   .

More to be desired are they than
    gold,
sweeter also than honey
    and drippings of the honeycomb.
                    —Pss. 119:16; 19:7-10

Second, now in the light of this Eternal Goodness turn and look at the things you are most afraid of losing, for back of these you will find your sins. "I cannot live without my John (or my Mary)." "I don't want to live unless I can have my health—my way—my money—my recognition." See that no matter how good these self-idols are, they are not good enough to be your God. They are indeed in their very compulsiveness your sin, for they shut you out from the larger good which God waits to give you.

Third, turn these compulsive demands loose; *Let go* and *let God!*

Lord Jesus, I long to be perfectly whole;
I want Thee forever to live in my soul;
Break down every idol, cast out every foe;
Now wash me, and I shall be whiter than snow.

.   .   .   .

Lord Jesus, thou seest I patiently wait;
Come now, and within me a new heart create;
To those who have sought Thee, Thou never said'st "No";
Now wash me, and I shall be whiter than snow.
                            —James Nicholson

3. COURAGEOUSLY I GROW THROUGH MY IMPERFECTIONS TOWARD MATURITY

The prayer of honest confession before the loving reality of God and his truth is like opening the door into a dark, stale room and letting in the light and fresh air. Once the door is open, you wonder why you remained in the darkness for so long!

Honest confession before God is the only way to deal with idolatry of self with its resulting fears and hates, inadequacies and hostilities. For as we have seen, we never rid ourselves of these disturbing and destructive symptoms until we deal adequately with the cause: "The dark idolatry of self," as Shelley calls it.

In this sense each one of us is a sinner. That is we have an idealized picture of ourselves—a false self—which we are trying to achieve. We can never achieve it because it is not according to reality (God's will). Therefore, we are subject to what Karen Horney calls *"The tyranny of the should"* or what may be called *The Dark Prison of the Must-haves*. This idealized self says to you and me over and over: "You should be smart enough to understand everything, strong enough to do anything, good enough to be anything you want to be. You must always be liked. You must win your way by your superiority. You should be perfect in your body, your looks, your success, in the eyes of others."

But you and I are not that smart! Only God could be as smart or as strong or as perfect as I want to be! This is my sin: wanting to be as God, instead of accepting myself as one of God's creatures, trusting and obeying the truth, I set up my goal of perfection and lose my life trying to reach it. But since I am not always liked or admired, superior, succeeding, considered tops, secure, comfortable, healthy, happy, I am anxious about my shortcomings. I am afraid of failure. And sooner or later I begin to dislike or even hate myself for being so dumb, so inept, so imperfect, so unsuccessful. And I seek to punish myself with guilt feelings or self-inflicted pain. And what is even worse, I transfer my self-hatred on to others who have "shown me up" or gotten in my way. From this sin all the deadly sins come. According to Jesus there is only one sin: seeking to save your false, proud self. All of the attitudes and acts generally regarded as "sins" are the children of this parent "Sin"— spelled with a capital "S"!

Oh, somehow I manage to keep going by justifying and excusing myself and blaming others, but living is a pretty difficult business. A little success puffs me up. A little failure casts me down. So much of the time when you and I are in the Dark Prison House of the Must-haves, we are miserable, exhausted, afraid, hostile, failing. Describing this useless suffering, Meister Eckhart comments on the words from *Theologia Germanica:*

"The only thing that burns in hell is self-will." I should say that because God and all who live in his presence have something like true blessedness in them, such as those who are cut off from God have not, it is only the "Not" (—the need or want of blessing) that punishes souls in hell, rather than any willfulness or other kind of fuel. Truly I say that to the extent "Not" exists in you, you are imperfect, and if you would be perfect you must get rid of it. . . .

The moment you get (one of your own) ideas, God fades out. . . . It is when the idea is gone that God gets in.[8]

What a blessed release to bow in the presence of the all-knowing and all-wise love of God to surrender this dark idolatry of self, with all its false "not-ideas" willing at last to be just what I am in God's sight, no more and no less! What freedom to say with another man who suffered "the tyranny of the should" and gave up in despair before finding at last the new creation "in Christ:"

Wretched man that I am! Who will deliver me from this body of death? Thanks be to God through Jesus Christ our Lord! . . . Yet whatever gain I had, I counted as loss for the sake of Christ. Indeed I count everything as loss because of the surpassing worth of knowing Christ Jesus my Lord. . . . and be found in him, not having a righteousness of my own, . . . but that which is through faith in Christ. . . . Brethren, I do not consider that I . . . [am perfect]; but one thing I do, forgetting what lies behind and straining forward to what lies ahead, I press on toward the goal for the prize of the upward call of God in Christ Jesus. Let those of us who are mature be thus minded.

—Rom. 7:24-25; Phil. 3:7-9, 13-15

For "the worth of knowing Christ Jesus my Lord" is the worth of being able to accept myself with all my imperfections, surrendering "a righteousness of my own" (that is, my own ways of being perfect) and pressing on toward the goal of a mature man or woman "in Christ Jesus."

This is the longing expressed in the Collect for Purity:

Almighty God, unto whom all hearts are open, all desires known, and from whom no secrets are hid [before whom dishonesty, rationalizations, self-justifications are useless]; cleanse the thoughts of our hearts by the inspiration of thy holy Spirit, that we may perfectly love thee, and worthily magnify thy holy name; through Jesus Christ our Lord. Amen.[9]

Perfectly to love God and his purposes for us is the only kind of perfection permitted us as creaturely children. It is a perfection of growth. As the green apple in June is as perfect for June as the ripe-red apple is for October, so I am able to confess my finitude and imperfection, accept myself as I am, and grow toward maturity.

Yes, Lord, I am faulty and full of imperfection. There is only one perfection I may have on earth: a perfection of heart, of intention, of longing that my soul may be whole. But my knowledge is imperfect and the drag of past experiences is written in my unconscious mind; therefore my ability to act and think and speak perfectly always falls short.

I come before thee, O God, whose love and mercy I see in Christ.

> Dear Master, in whose life I see
> All that I would, but fail to be;
> Let Thy clear light forever shine,
> To shame and guide this life of mine.
> —JOHN HUNTER

To shame me? Yes, but only enough to help me see the false and be ready and willing to be guided into the true possibilities for my life. Thus the honest, sincere prayer of confession saves me from proud self-love or from proud self-dejection. I am able to grow "to mature manhood, to the measure of the stature of the fullness of Christ." Then the self I love is the true self which God loves.

There is no more interesting or inspiring biography of spiritual growth than that of Brother Lawrence, a wonderful Christian of seventeenth-century France who found his growth in maturity as a dishwasher in a monastery through what he calls "The Practice of the Presence of God." No doubt his self-idol was hurt often when he first began, as the cook hurled a pot at him and cursed him. No doubt he said as you and I have said, "I should be out of this." No doubt he struggled with resentment and hatred for his lowly circumstances as well as for the unkindness of those who sought to elevate themselves by making him feel little. But he tells us of the way he grew:

I have no pain or difficulty about my state, because I have no will but that of God, which I endeavor to accomplish in all things, and to which I am so resigned that I would not take up a straw from the ground against His order, or for any other motive than purely that of love to Him. . . .

I think it proper to inform you after what manner I consider myself before God. . . .

I consider myself as the most wretched of men [that is, imperfect and faulty], full of sores and corruption, and who has committed all sorts of crimes against his King [that is, against his real self as God, the King, sees it]. Touched with a sensible regret, I confess to Him all my wickedness [it is wicked to keep an impossible goal and fail of the good and

41

beautiful which is my potential], I ask this forgiveness, I abandon myself in His hands that He may do what He pleases with me. The King, full of mercy and goodness, very far from chastising me, embraces me with love, makes me eat at His table, serves me with His own hands, gives me the keys of His treasures; . . . in a thousand and a thousand ways, [He blesses me].[10]

All of this was the result of honest, adoring prayer of confession: acceptance in the love of God, imperfect but growing. He continues: "Sometimes I consider myself there as a stone before a carver whereof he is to make a statue; presenting myself thus before God, I desire Him to form His perfect image in my soul, and make me entirely like Himself."[11] This does not mean that he considered himself perfect or as one who performed his work perfectly.

In his work he continued his familiar conversation with his Maker, . . . offering to Him all his actions. . . . When he had finished he examined himself how he had discharged his duty; if he found well, he returned thanks to God; if otherwise, he asked pardon, and without being discouraged, he set his mind right again, and continued his exercise of the presence of God, as if he had never deviated from it. "Thus," said he, "by rising after my falls, and by frequently renewed acts of faith and love, I am come to a state wherein it would be as difficult for me not to think of God as it was at first to accustom myself to it."[12]

In conclusion, let me suggest four ways to find this freedom in prayer:

Confess and admit your failures, as well as symptoms—hold back not honest so far as you are able to be.

Accept God's loving forgiveness no you did which you should not have the things you should have done but didn't.

Do not beat and abuse yourself for being imperfect, but take your imperfections and accept them as part of your human limitations. Seek to grow out of them where they are caused by your failure to see and accept God's will. Be impatient with the false only long enough to see and deny it and to accept the true. Forgive yourself even as God has forgiven you, and without being discouraged set your mind right in the presence of God and continue to grow!

Then rest your life and all your desires and needs peacefully, truthfully, thankfully in God's presence. How to do this latter will be the burden of much that follows.

"Grant me, dear Lord, the serenity to accept the things I cannot change, the courage to change what I can and the wisdom to know the difference."

"Not what I would but what I can I offer Thee, O Lord."

"Have Thine own way, Lord! Have Thine own way!
Thou art the Potter; I am the clay.
Mold me and make me After Thy will,
While I am waiting, Yielded and still."

III. COMMITMENT

1. GLADLY I ACCEPT A CREATIVE
PARTNERSHIP WITH GOD

Prayer at its highest level is the commitment of my little, failing, imperfect mind and heart and will to love and work with the mighty mind and will of the Eternal God. The results of such prayer are magnificent beyond all description.

Over against this tremendous privilege, however, is the amazing fact of our human freedom to defy God. I who am physically but a speck of protoplasm on one of the smallest planets, nevertheless, have the power to deny, resist, resent, and oppose the mighty purposes of God. No other creature on earth has this power. No plant, animal, atom, star, or universe can defy its Creator. All move in humble obedience to the mind that made them. "The sun rises every morning," said G. K. Chesterton, "because God says 'Get up.'" But I who am given the power to think and to choose, to believe myself made with some genuine correspondence with God, I alone can defy him, fight him, say "no" to him and his great purposes.

The only freedom I do not have is the freedom to

escape the resulting suffering and failure of my rejection.

Prayer is the exact opposite of such proud and foolish rebellion. We may also voluntarily and gladly say "yes" to the Mighty Goodness. In adoration we recognize the infinite and steadfast love of God in Christ in whom we believe is the clue to the nature of God. In honest confession we recognize the folly of seeking to save our little self-gods. In wholehearted commitment we dedicate ourselves to accept the will of God and to work with him in every way we can discover. When you pray, taught Jesus, say:

> Thy kingdom come.
> Thy will be done,
> on earth as it is in heaven.

The noblest act of human life is to become a conscious part of the creative fellowship and work of God. Not a "partner" in the literal sense that we are equals; but in the realistic sense that we are "partakers of the divine nature" and part-takers in the work of God. "For we are fellow workmen for God; you are God's field, God's building." (I Cor. 3:9.)

There is unimaginable power in this multi-universe. Enough power in a small handful of atoms to blow up a city or to push a great ship through the ocean for months at a time. Power for creation and renewal of our expanding universe and growing minds.

The power of a jet plane is the result of the prayer of ten thousand scientists, technicians, mechanics, and a pilot who say "yes" together to the harmonies of God's will in aerodynamics.

The power of a rocket zooming thousands of miles into space is the result of prayer, the "yes" to God's mighty plan by tens of thousands of scientists, engineers, and spacemen. Watch the scientists laboring to perfect their co-operation in order to say their "yes" more completely. As the rocket takes off, they say breathlessly, "There she goes," and if they are sensitive at all, they add, "Thank God." For it is God whose mysterious and magnificent will is being fulfilled.

Each of these say, "Have Thine own way, Lord," in the physical universe.

The deepest and most necessary prayer of all, however, is the surrendered will of man in his personal and social universe to love and serve and give and live in the Spirit of Christ—to fulfill the will of God "on earth as it is fulfilled in heaven." To be "in the kingdom of heaven" according to Jesus is to begin to realize the fullest and best good that God the Heavenly Father has for his children. It would be to pray:

Have thine own way, Lord, so we do not send these planes and jets screaming to destruction. Grant us as we work with thee the power to discover peace!

Have thine own way, that thy love and peace may come to all mankind, so that we may all be one in thy family and that each may be accorded the dignity and opportunity thou has planned for all. Grant us the power for love.

Have thine own way, Lord, that thy loving presence and power may live in my heart—Grant me power to win over hate and fear, jealously and lust, envy and greed, and the self-idols that produce them!

In the final analysis we get over our fears and irritations, our weakness and folly only as we lose ourselves in a wholehearted commitment that says, "Have Thine own way, Lord." Or to put it in other words, "Lord, keep me on the beam!"

Here is a nervously exhausted and distraught man, broken in health and in spirit. His name is John Henry Newman. He has attempted to be a minister in the church, but his ego-idols are too great for him to conquer. His prayers are empty and his leading of worship is only a form. One day in the presence of the "kindly light" of God in Christ he makes a prayer of commitment which unites him with the healing, life-giving powers of God. He becomes one of the most dynamic Christians of his time. This is the prayer he prayed:

Make me what Thou wouldst have me; I bargain for nothing; I make no terms; I seek for no previous information whither Thou art taking me; I will be what Thou wilt make me, and all Thou wilt make me. I say not, I will follow Thee whithersoever Thou goest, for I am weak; but I give myself to Thee to lead me anywhither.

No wonder his great hymn, "Lead, Kindly Light," has inspired so many. The secret of its power is in the second stanza:

I was not ever thus, nor prayed that Thou
  Should lead me on;
I loved to choose and see my path; but now

Lead Thou me on!
I loved the garish day, and, spite of fears,
Pride ruled my will: remember not past years!

"*Lead Thou me on!*" Here is another man named John Wesley who at the age of thirty-five was a conscious failure, having done everything he knew how to do to make himself righteous and adequate. Coming back from America where he had gone as a missionary to the Indians, he was broken in health and spirit. Then he too found this highest level of prayer. Before he had been concerned to exalt himself as "the most holy man," but one who must have his own comfort first, unwilling to take a little church because he could not bear to be away from the inspiration of his companions at Oxford. Now he prays in the simple commitment of another before him:

O Lord, thou knowest what is best for us, let this or that be done as thou pleasest.

Give what thou wilt, and how much thou wilt, and when thou wilt. . . .

Set me where thou wilt, and deal with me in all things just as thou wilt.

I am in thy hand: turn me round, and turn me back again, as thou shalt please.

Behold, I am thy servant, prepared for all things; for I desire not to live unto myself, but unto thee; and O that I could do it worthily and perfectly.[1]

Now he is in partnership with the Lord—"not a slave but a son in his father's house!" His life was one of amazing endurance and creative power. His prayer was a continuing "yes" to the will of God!

Herein is the secret of thousands of Alcoholics Anonymous all over the world who learn to pray with adoration, confession, and commitment, "turning our lives over to God as we understand him." Their prayer is effective within the fellowship of other alcoholics who are winning the same victory through saying "yes" to God's loving purposes of harmony and joy. Most of them have prayed many times before and nothing happened, because usually they were praying only for removal of their symptoms. Now they pray with John Henry Newman, John Wesley, and every other victor in life, as you and I pray in this present moment:

God, I offer myself to thee—to build with me and to do with me as thou wilt. Relieve me of the bondage of self, that I may better do thy will. Take away my self-willed difficulties that victory over them may bear witness to those I would help of thy power, thy love, and thy way of life. May I do thy will this hour, this day, and then I will be able to do it increasingly with joy and victory each day thereafter!

2. "IF WITH ALL YOUR HEARTS YE TRULY SEEK ME"

I often say my prayers,
But do I ever pray;
And do the wishes of my heart
Go with the words I say?

I may as well kneel down
And worship gods of stone,
As offer to the living God
A prayer of words alone.

For words without the heart
The Lord will never hear:
Nor will he to those lips attend
Whose prayers are not sincere.[2]
—JOHN BURTON

When is prayer sincere, resulting in new and precious power to live and serve well? Certainly not when it is primarily words or forms. Nor when it is fleeting, casual wishing. Prayer is not begging, nor first of all asking. Sincere prayer that results in power for the best and highest in me and in my world is a wholehearted seeking of God with the deepest desires and longings, the strongest passions of my life.

If with all your hearts ye truly seek me,
Ye shall ever surely find me. Thus saith our God.[3]

Wholehearted means healthy-hearted. "To be pure in heart is to will one thing," wrote Kierkegaard. It means going in one direction rather than several. Too many of us are like the cowboy who got on his horse and rode off in all directions. His horsemanship was not very healthy, and he didn't go very far. Neither do we in a divided life, for a divided heart is a very sick one.

On the other hand when I spend a minute or a half-hour consciously with all my heart going in the direction of God, I find God's light and life with increasing strength and reality.

> Whoso draws nigh to God one step
>   through doubtings dim,
> God will advance a mile
>   in blazing light to him.[4]
>   —AUTHOR UNKNOWN

But you do not go even an inch toward God, except with your whole heart.

What is it to be wholehearted and how do you get that way? To be *whole*-hearted is the opposite of *half*-hearted. The *heart* is a symbol of the center of desire which alone has the power to move the will. There is no such thing as a "weak will." The will is always moved by the strongest desires. This great promise from the Bible could be paraphrased thus: If with all your deepest desires and strongest passions and your sincerest love that move your mightiest will, you seek me, you shall ever truly find me, thus saith the Lord. It is clear that any half-hearted quest for God and his truth will never succeed in doing anything more than making us miserable.

Henry Nelson Wieman puts the same truth in this figure of speech: You never really pray or worship until you "go out into deep water" any more than one learns how to swim by putting one foot into the water at a time or by staying in the shallows. One learns to swim when he commits himself wholly to the water and discovers that through his co-operation and trust the water will bear him up. Kierkegaard, using the same figure, says the trouble with most of us who seek to pray is that we are like the fellow who hangs himself up by his belt from the ceiling and mistakes the animated motion of his arms and limbs for swimming.

How do you swim? Not by putting the toe or the knee or even the body up to the chin in the water, but only by casting oneself out into the deep water that is over one's head in which one cannot save himself by touching the bottom. So we pray only when we cast away our deepest desires and wants and trust our lives to the sustaining power of the will of God which does bear us up. There is as much difference in "saying prayers" and praying as there is in practicing strokes on the beach and in swimming.

Put these tests to your prayers. What is my deepest level of desiring? What is it I really love and want the most? What is my master passion? That is my prayer whatever it is—"the soul's sincere desire, unuttered or expressed." Do I want God and his truth and way with all my heart? Or do I merely want God's gifts of peace and strength to add to and bolster up my ego-idol? Am I willing really to depend on God? To do his will completely as best I understand it? Or am I still trying to depend on myself, and if I pray at all, to get the Mighty Power of the Universe hitched up to the success of my idealized-self picture?

Augustine had prayed in the latter way with no results in life or victory. "O God make me chaste and continent, but not yet!" It was only when he prayed, "Thy will be done, now," that he found the beginnings of a creative life of love and truth.

David Head has suggested the way some of our prayers would sound if the deepest desires of our unconscious minds were put into words—words that certainly would contradict the spoken words we use so piously on Sunday morning. For instance, this litany:

We miserable owners of increasingly luxurious cars, and ever-expanding television screens, do most humbly pray for that two-thirds of the world's population which is under-nourished;
    You can do all things, O God.

We who seek to maintain a shaky civilization do pray most earnestly that the countries which suffer exploitation may not be angry with the exploiters, that the hungry may not harbour resentment against those who have food, that the down-trodden may take it patiently, that nations with empty larders may prefer starvation to communism, . . . that all people who have been deeply insulted and despised may have short memories;
    You can do all things, O God.[5]

Yes, God can do all things—except to deny his love and justice; and he will not answer the prayer of our lips when our heart's desire offers a contradictory prayer. Sometimes he will do as Ps. 106 suggests he did with the Israelites:

> They soon forgat his works;
> They waited not for his counsel,
> But lusted exceedingly in the
>   wilderness,
> And tempted God in the desert.

And he gave them request,
But sent leanness into their soul.
—Ps. 106:13-15 A.S.V.

Sometimes God answers our "soul's sincere desire" with a "yes" even when we are asking for the wrong thing, but sends "leanness into their soul," or "a wasting disease" that keeps us inadequate for life. Why? Because only thus can we learn to change our desires from the false to the real!

Most of us can understand the devious kind of praying illustrated by the college sophomore who regularly touched his knees to the floor before retiring as though to say, "God I want you to be with me in danger or difficulty, and this is to keep you on my side." We too have prayed, "Thy kingdom come, but not yet!"

John Oxenham puts the conditions of effective Christian prayer clearly:

> Who answers Christ's insistent call
> Must give himself, his life, his all,
> Without one backward look.
> Who sets his hand unto the plow,
> And glances back with anxious brow,
> His calling hath mistook.
> Christ claims him wholly for His own;
> He must be Christ's, and Christ's alone.[6]

Thus I am brought up sharp at the crossroads. I either commit myself wholeheartedly to discover and fulfill the truth of my being, utterly willing to do the good will of God because I long for it as a drowning man longs for air or a blind man longs for light; or I turn back to half-way house in which my faith in God is multiplied con-fusion, futility itself. If the latter is my desire then though I am outwardly

> Living, and [there is] no life in me?
> [I] languish in expectancy?—
> Dying to my dying day.

Instead let me decide as of now that what I truly want most is to be alive even though it means dying to my little self-idol. Let it go! It must! I hate it! I love the Lord with all my heart and soul and mind and body and strength!

> Thou mastering me
> God! giver of breath and bread;
> World's strand, sway of the sea;
> Lord of living and dead;
> Thou hast bound bones and veins in me, fastened me flesh,
> And after it almost unmade, what with dread,
> Thy doing: and dost thou touch me afresh?
> Over again I feel thy finger and find thee.

. . . .

> Be adored among men,

. . . .

> Wring thy rebel, dogged in den,

. . . .

> Beyond saying sweet, past telling of tongue,
> Thou art lightning and love, I found it, a winter and warm;

Father and fondler of heart thou hast wrung:

. . . .

I admire thee, master of the tides,
Of the Yore-flood, of the years fall.[7]
—GERARD MANLEY HOPKINS

I give myself to thee, "Thou mastering me God." I want thee most! I love Thee best!

"Accept, O Lord, my entire liberty, my memory, my understanding and my will. All that I am and have Thou hast given me; and I give all back to Thee to be disposed of according to Thy good pleasure. Give me only the comfort of Thy Presence and the joy of Thy love; with these I shall be more than rich and shall desire nothing more." [8]

IV. PETITION

1. THE PRIMARY LESSON OF
MIDNIGHT PRAYERS

When wholeheartedly I pray:

> Thy kingdom come,
> Thy will be done,

I am ready to enter into a creative partnership with God. This puts an entirely different light on prayer. In Paul Wellman's The Chain, Gilda the young sophisticate is asked by Carlisle the young pastor, "Do you believe in prayer?" Deciding to be candid she answered what she considered to be his ridiculous question by saying:

"I'm afraid not much. Asking God for favors isn't an occupation that appeals to me. I believe that you'll get what's coming to you, good or bad, and any amount of praying won't change it."

"That's not the kind of prayer I mean."

"Then what?"

His eyes again were burning. "I mean prayer which asks for nothing; the upthrusting of the soul, perhaps entirely wordless—seeking only direct experience with God; a naked intent to God alone and not to anything He has made; the concentration of the whole being on finding God and knowing Him.[1]

The story continues with Gilda growing sick by the superficiality of her life—the formal prayers, the meaningless worship when she did go to church. In a time of personal crisis she found her way one summer to a lonely place in the Rocky Mountains where her whole soul went out to God. She found him and was found by him. Then prayer became for her the door to a meaningful and worthy life.

This does not mean that we should not pray about particular things and needs, but that becomes secondary —always a wholesome and priceless by-product of the prayer of dedication.

"If you abide in me, and my words abide in you, ask whatever you will, and it shall be done for you." (John 15:7.) This is the primary lesson Jesus sought to teach in his often misunderstood parables of the men who knocked at midnight for bread for a hungry friend and the unjust judge who though he neither feared God nor regarded man granted the poor widow's plea because of her persistence lest she weary him. In both of these parables Jesus is contrasting God with the unjust judge and the selfish neighbor who grumblingly gets out of bed to provide bread for his neighbor's hungry friend. God is not like this growling, grudging friend who finally comes to your aid only because of your begging or like the stubborn and unjust judge who answers your cry because of your persistence.

This is the very point Jesus makes clear in these words:

So I tell you, ask and it will be given you, search and you will find, knock and the door will be opened to you. The one who asks will always receive; the one who is searching will always find, and the door is opened to the man who knocks. Some of you are fathers, and if your son asks you for some fish would you give him a snake instead, or if he asks you for an egg would you make him a present of a scorpion? So, if you, for all your evil, know how to give good things to your children, how much more likely is it that your Heavenly Father will give the Holy Spirit to those who ask him!

—Luke 11:9-13 Phillips

Since God is much more willing to give than we are to ask, we cannot ask too urgently. Persistence in prayer is vastly important, but we may persist in the wrong way. We are not to ask, seek, and knock in order to batter down the resistance of a reluctant God to get our needs and the needs of those about us met, but our persistence is needed to fit us to receive the best gifts which God is waiting to give!

We need first to understand the difference between prayer and magic, a difference all of us have missed at times. The witch doctor's incantations and the way many of us pray vary only in words and methods not in spirit. "If I pray long enough, using just the right words and phrases, God will have to give me what I want." "If I deny and punish myself enough, God will finally hear and help me." But God is not at our bidding! Who among us with all his smart phrases or long prayers can command the Almighty! To attempt to do so is calling on magic and not faith!

Persistence in prayer is needed not to bend God's will to ours but to bend our wills to his. We need the persistence of the neighbor who knocks at midnight and the widow who keeps coming to the judge until they receive what they need. But for a different reason: not because God is reluctant or indifferent, but because we must find the way to open up our lives to his beauty and truth and thus to receive the gifts which he is waiting to shower upon us. *Christian prayer is not magic to control God.* It is loving communion and fellowship with him through which he can give us the Holy Spirit to control and lead us in the pathway of noble, joyous living!

Therefore says Leon Bloy, "The only sorrow is not to be a saint!" For a saint is a person who is committed to God's truth and able to receive the insight, courage, and love which gives adequate light even at midnight. Not to be this kind of person, this is the only sorrow—not the midnight circumstances, however difficult.

All of us have had or will have midnight prayers. The darkness is formidable. My future is as impenetrable as the blackness of the night. I am caught between the unrelenting jaws of demands too great for my small powers. And so I come to God just as the man came at midnight to his friend asking for bread. I ask, seek, knock. I cry:

> Thy sea, O God, so great,
>   My boat so small.
> It cannot be that any happy fate
>   Will me befall
> Save as Thy goodness opens paths for me
> Through the consuming vastness of the sea.

Thy winds, O God, so strong,
   So slight my sail.

. . . .

Thy world, O God, so fierce,
   And I so frail.[2]
       —WINFRED ERNEST GARRISON

But it is not the greatness of the seas, the fierceness of the world, or the terror of the wind that is my real sorrow: *It is rather the fact that I am not able to accept the Holy Spirit who could make me able for anything. The only sorrow is not to be a saint!*

That is why I have to keep asking, seeking, and knocking: in order to open the door to him who waits to enter with bread for all my needs and my neighbor's as well.

This I have learned at midnight. I have had many disappointments and seeming failures in my life; but none of them were really bad for me except the ones wherein I was so filled with self-pity, resentment, and fear caused by my ego-idols that I could not receive the precious gift of the spirit waiting for me.

I have learned that when I ask for understanding, for wisdom, for insight in order that I may fulfill God's will —the real purpose for my life—I receive it.

I have learned that when I seek and knock for courage, strength, and adequacy to be at my best in the fulfillment of my true mission, I always find the door opened with power to use my talents in a more remarkable way than I ever imagined.

This is not only my testimony but the witness of countless thousands of ordinary persons as well as those whom the world calls extraordinary. The greatest achievements are not always to those with the most natural talents but to those whose prayers are the open doors to the full use of the small talent they may possess.

One of my friends is a distinguished Texan artist, Merrit Mauzey, who has received the Guggenheim Fellowship Award and numerous other prizes in recognition of his work. I cherish a letter he wrote to me back in 1952 in which he expressed the key to his success in art:

It has been prayer. Before doing a picture I always invoke the aid of the Lord, and without that my talent would have been wasted. Before creating, I pray earnestly that my talent may be used constructively. Part of that prayer was answered when the Metropolitan Museum honored the print, but it was ten years later that the full fruition of that prayer came into being. I have had this happen over and over again; therefore, I am never disappointed when my prayer is not immediately answered. As I write this letter I am blinded with tears of happiness that the Lord has seen fit to use the talent with which he has entrusted me.

Therefore ask and you always will receive, if you are asking to receive the Holy Spirit of new life in Christ! In the words of a dear friend of mine, an elementary public school teacher, Mrs. Wayne Holmes, let us also pray:

> To God I give my hands, my heart,
> For service here, to do my part.
> I ask forgiveness for my sin
> Through Jesus Christ, my Lord. Amen.

2. I ASK NOT, KEEP ME SAFE, BUT KEEP ME LOYAL

Prayer brings deliverance, but not always the way we are expecting it. All of us are familiar with stories of prayers that are claimed to have brought sudden safety in the midst of danger or need: a sea gull provides bait which Rickenbacker and his men used to catch fish, saving their lives until rescued; money appears for food and fuel when the last penny was gone; the rain comes to break a destructive drouth, or a wind blows the grasshoppers away from the crops.

These prayers are too naïve and unscientific, so many think. "How could prayer influence a bird or the wind or the rain?" they ask. "These are subject to 'natural laws' which all the praying on earth will not change." On the other hand those who believe in this kind of praying would add, "That is unless prayer itself is one of the primary 'natural laws' as we believe it is!" So the argument runs. But here is obviously no place for an extended debate over *The Power of Prayer on Plants* as the title of one book reads, or the power of prayer over animals, things, natural laws. There is plenty of evidence that can be used on both sides of the argument. Such discussion may be helpful to some, but is repellent to others, and must not be permitted to sidetrack the earnest seeker after what for him is an intelligible approach to Christian prayer. Of primary significance to every one of us is the honest, adoring prayer of the committed, trusting heart that makes one a partner in a small but real way with the Creative Power of the universe.

For there is deliverance infinitely more important than in the change or removal of physical circumstances. There is the large number of alcoholics, lost on the sea of alcoholism, who have been delivered by prayer: "We . . . came to believe that a power greater than ourselves, could restore us to sanity. . . . [We] made a decision to turn our will and our lives over to the care of God as we understood Him." [3]

There is an even larger number of persons with a recognition of their helplessness on the great ocean of temptation, sorrow, and evil who through prayer also have found adequacy and victory in the worst circumstances.

A little girl, daughter of a missionary family in Sarawak, said when it came time for her to offer up her prayer in the family-prayer circle: "God give us strength. God give us courage!" That kind of prayer is always answered. This fact is repeated in the experience of countless persons in every age. In times of difficulty and suffering, God's help comes not merely through a providential sea gull, or some other remarkable thing that solves your problem, but through new courage and strength to meet the worst even when there is no sea gull!

Witnesses to this truth come in unexpected places. Read the warm and inspiring autobiography of Roy Campanella, famous Dodger catcher, entitled, *It's Good to Be Alive.* In it he tells how he came out of an automobile accident with a broken neck and a paralyzed body. After almost dying with pneumonia, he was at last able to see himself for the first time in a mirror. With tubes in this throat and nose, strapped to a bed which turned upside down to help his circulation, with Crutchfield tongs pulling at his head, he said: "I never felt so low . . . I cried, 'Lord have mercy on me.' I prayed." But it was a prayer of self-pity and his despondency grew worse. He refused to see anyone and insisted on the lights being shut out.

It was in the darkness that the worst thoughts . . . and fears . . . came. I couldn't chase them . . . at night, during those long hours when I was alone, I couldn't help thinking bad thoughts . . . I couldn't fight off fear.

What will become of me? Am I going to die? If I live will I be paralyzed and never walk again? Will I always be like this—helpless, unable to move. . . . And what about my family? Ruthie and the kids? . . . Over and over, those thoughts kept gnawing at me. . . . I lost interest in everything. I was filled with self-pity, with despair. . . . my brain full of panic . . . I know I cried myself to sleep many a night.

Then the doctor came and talked to him, saying that he expected him to put up a better fight than this.

"Roy," he said, "you've got to fight. We can only help you ten percent. The other ninety has to be your effort." . . . After he left, I began to think. I knew he was right. I had to start thinking right thoughts . . . I remembered my Bible. I asked the nurse . . . to get it . . . and open it to the Twenty-third Psalm: *The Lord is my shepherd. I shall not want . . . Yea, though I walk through the valley of death, I will fear no evil; for Thou art with me.* From that moment on, I was on my way back . . . I no longer felt sorry for myself. This was a little tough break that happened to me. But it was something I knew I could handle with the help of the good Lord.

It's quite a nice thing to have God on your side—and I know He is on mine.[4]

The simple but profound fact is that Campy's midnight prayers began to put him on God's side. He discovered the "how much more" of Jesus' promise. The book is a remarkable testimony of the creative power given this rugged ball player who, though he could catch no more for the Dodgers, was able to train their pitchers from a wheelchair. He has been an inspiration to hundreds of others. Since writing the book, Campy has had trouble in other ways. Whether he comes out a victor as in this first, great crisis depends on how well he prays. Campy's favorite poem is the words of a Confederate soldier found on the bronze memorial plaque riveted to the wall in the reception room of the Institute of Physical Medicine and Rehabilitation where Campy spent so many months:

I asked God for strength, that I might achieve
    I was made weak, that I might learn humbly to obey . . .

I asked for health, that I might do greater things
    I was given infirmity, that I might do better things . . .

I asked for riches, that I might be happy
    I was given poverty that I might be wise . . .

  . . . .

I asked for all things that I might enjoy life
    I was given life, that I might enjoy all things . . .

  . . . .

    I am among men, most richly blessed!

How much more God gives when we ask in humble, glad surrender to his purposes. When we ask in this spirit we can never ask too much.

The spiritual universe in which we live is infinitely more marvelous than we think. The power for loving, joyous, creative life is measureless and inexhaustible.

> What no eye has seen, nor ear
> heard,
> nor the heart of man conceived,
> what God has prepared for those
> who love him.
> —I Cor. 2:9

The trouble with us is we either ask too little or ask in the wrong way. "You do not have, because you do not ask" says the Letter of James. "You ask and do not receive, because you ask wrongly, to spend it on your passions."

> I asked for bread!
> Life led me to a plain,
> And put a plough at hand,
> And bade me toil until my bread I earned.

How much more desirable is the gift of bread earned than bread given. Toil is rewarding and blessed indeed when in the pathway of a glad and thankful purpose.

> I asked for drink!
> Life led me to a sand
> As dry as tearless grief—
> Forced me to find the springs of sympathy.

How much more desirable is love and sympathy than selfish pleasure. How much more blessed to give than to receive.

I asked for joy!
    Life led me to a street,
    And had me hear the cries
    Of wayward souls who waited to be freed.

How much more joy is there in freeing others than in seeking for the evanescent joys that leave one sated and bored.

I asked for words!
    Life led me to a wood,
    Set me in solitude
    Where speech is still and wisdom comes by prayer.

How much better is the wisdom of solitude than the power of easy but foolish words which leave my ego exalted only for a moment and cause me to miss the greater power of wise utterance.

I asked for love!
    Life led me to a hill,
    And bound me to a cross
    To bear and lift and be hanged upon.[5]

But the cross I feared becomes my greatest opportunity; for I enter into the joy of my Lord and find the power of loving by which life is significant and death is triumphant!

Yes, "how much more" will your Heavenly Father give when you ask rightly even in pain and death. I have been inspired as have countless others by the testimony of a noble German Christian, Otto Carl Kiep, who before his execution as a victim of Nazism wrote his profession of faith: "This is the meaning of prayer: to summon one's best strength in humility: to gain a sense of perspective in which all things are rightly seen; to stop doing what one has begun foolishly; and to place one's trust in the guidance of Him who is on high." [6]

This is indeed the priceless meaning of prayer—the victory of the Spirit over all circumstances, even death.

A glorious company of sainted souls
Have stood in every age alone with Thee
To wrest from earthquake's havoc and the coals
A new world and a nobler destiny.
I hear Thee, Lord, above the sound of strife,
More gleaming in Thy greatness than the fire;
Let my small voice in stillness speak Thy life,
Its whisper blending in Thy mighty choir;
And from unstirred quiescence grant release,
That through the noise and fire may come Thy peace. [7]
—GEORGIA HARKNESS

For this is the precious heritage of faith in which we may share and we pray, through this ancient prayer found in W. E. Orchard's book *The Kingdom, the Power and the Glory:*

Help us daily to know more of thee, and through us by the power of thy spirit, show forth thyself to others. Make us humble, brave and loving. Make us ready for adventure.

We do not ask that thou wilt keep us safe, but that thou wilt keep us loyal: who for us didst face death unafraid and dost live and reign forever and ever!

3. WHAT THEN SHOULD I PRAY FOR AND WHAT GOOD WILL IT DO?

Should I not pray, then, for deliverance? For food, material, and other specific things I need? Of course. Jesus underlined this when he included in his prayer the petition, "Give us this day our daily bread."

We must begin with our felt needs—wherever we are. For we must be honest, or prayer is useless. If in anger or bitterness, self-pity or despair, or selfish desire for things that are really unnecessary or in my human longing for deliverance from trouble and pain—if this is where I am, then this is where I must begin praying! Jesus also felt the pangs of hunger and the threats of pain and humiliation as evidenced by his prayers in the Wilderness and in Gethsemane, "Father, all things are possible to thee, remove this cup from me."

The one thing that matters is how our prayer ends. Do I finish my searching quest by asking longingly, trustingly, "Thy will be done!" That is the real test of my prayer: not where it begins, but where does it end? "The real question," says Douglas Steere, "is, Were you faithful? Did you yield?"

Deliverance comes in God's own time and way when I pray not to be kept safe, but to be loyal! Loyal to the mighty purposes that seek expression through me! Loyal to the spirit of love that waits to make all people one family! "Courage is fear that has said its prayer." * Prayer begins in fear, worry, anxiety, resentment—"Give us safety," but when it ends in surrender, love, and trust, the result is courage! This courage is the best gift of all!

The following lines were inspired by the above words * of Earle Baker Wilson:

> Courage is fear that has said its prayer;
> Courage is faith that brave men share.
> Courage is meaning in the darkest night;
> Courage is hope in the hardest fight.
>
> Courage is joy in the fiercest struggle,
> Knowing God waits within the trouble,
> Sure that victory is in the right,
> Confident all is within his sight!
>
> Courage is fear that has said its prayer:
> Courage the faith that good men wear.
> The light of Christ that shows the way—
> Hope in Thee—an endless day!
>
> —LANCE WEBB

This still, however, does not answer our practical question: should I pray when I need new clothes or a different job? Should I pray about my future-expected in the choice of a mate? When I am in trouble? Before an examination?

The simplest answer to be found in the New Testament is in I Thess. 5:16-18: "Rejoice always, pray constantly, give thanks in all circumstances; for this is the will of God in Christ Jesus for you."

To pray for specifics is contrary to a growing feeling among many Christians who have revolted, and rightly, against the kind of self-centered praying that amounts to a system of magic in which one tries to use God for his own ends. Prayer is communion with God, and therefore they decide their asking should be limited to petition for courage and wisdom and never for specific things.

As has been pointed out the refusal to pray for that which we need is contrary to the teachings of Jesus and of Paul: "Give us this day our daily bread." "Pray constantly, give thanks in all circumstances."

You are to pray about everything: nothing is too small or unimportant to bring before your heavenly Father. If it concerns you, it concerns the One who seeks to help you grow into the magnificent person intended in your creation. "Even the hairs of your head are all numbered," said Jesus. "Fear not, therefore; you are of more value than many sparrows." (Matt. 10:30-31.)

Faced with this seeming contradiction, we must ask again, how should I pray about my problems and needs and what good will it do?

First, you are to "rejoice always." That is you put yourself in focus as precious in the sight of God, confident that there is always a way out, that his good is awaiting you if you are ready to find it. "My heart is ready, O God," therefore "I will sing." I am ready to believe in the infinite good that never fails even though I cannot see it. I am ready to love as I am loved. Now, Lord, about this need which seems so pressing!

This kind of prayer in any kind of circumstances does two things for you: (a) It takes the bitterness and gloom out; (b) it clears the air and makes best choice understandable and acceptable. Jane Merchant's beautiful experience describes this truth:

> Sometimes, perplexed and shaken,
> Uncertain of His will,
> In dread lest my mistaken
> Unguided act bring ill,
>
> I find I've been remiss
> In the one thing I must do:
> "Rejoice, give thanks, for this
> Is the will of God for you."
>
> So, letting go the worry
> That made my spirit dim,
> The pressure and the hurry,
> I offer praise to him
>
> In fullness of thanksgiving
> That he who keeps our days
> Wills that each hour of living
> Be full of joy and praise.
>
> And while my heart rejoices
> In his great love, I find
> The hard, perplexing choices
> Grow clear within my mind.[8]

Petition with rejoicing, adoration, and thanksgiving enables you to pray for the things you need in the right way. Consider these illustrations:

The exam you are preparing to take. The wrong way to pray is to say: "Lord, I may have been careless. I haven't studied, please give me the knowledge I sorely need and let me have an 'A' anyway." Such a prayer is a futile hokus pokus! The right way would be to pray something like this: "Lord, you have given me a good mind, I haven't used it as I should. I confess I have wasted much time. I have been lazy; now help me to use these hours to the best of my ability. Your will is for me to fulfill my highest potential. I trust you to help me and from now on I will use my time more appropriately!" Such a prayer will give you a clear brain and you will do twice as well as otherwise with what you know and next time you will be prepared!

The talk you are to give. You may pray, "Lord, help me to knock their eyes out, prove what a smart person I am—what a good speaker—and I will be elected to some high office or get a promotion." But you should pray, "Lord, how glad I am that you have given me the ability to speak! Here is something needing to be said, and people who need to understand it. Let me lose myself in my message." This latter prayer results in loss of timidity, a clear mind, and a convincing speech.

The sale you want to make. You pray, "Lord, you've got to help me—I must be rich, successful. I've got to pay for the car and the house. I must not lose this sale." Your prayer is wasted breath. But suppose instead you pray, "Lord, this person I am to see is a person precious in your sight. Help me to see him as he is with the same wants and needs I have and to respect him. Yes, I do need to make this sale. I need the money to pay for the car

and the house, but more than anytl.   -
true member of your family." This p.
swered in a new concern for your custome
understand him. You will come nearer ma.   ...e
than with the compulsive anxiety of the first prayer. And
whether you make the sale or not you will enter a closer,
more wholesome relationship with another person.

Maybe the problem is in your office: jealousy, bitterness, conflict. You pray for the troublemaker, whether
boss or fellow employee, in the spirit of humble willingness to see your part of the trouble, desiring real understanding both of the other person and of yourself, willing
to go the second mile or the third or the tenth to help
the other, and your prayer will be answered: (a) by
removing the threat the other has over you—your little
self is surrendered; (b) by giving you ability to do the
right thing even when the other does wrong; (c) by your
receiving the power to love the other even though you do
not like what he or she does.

So with the problem in your home or church or community or nation: Prayer changes things—you first, then
through you and your prayers the person for whom you
pray. How this latter takes place must be reserved for
the section on intercessory prayer which follows. But
that it does happen is the glad witness of every age!

Therefore, "rejoice always, pray constantly, give thanks
in all circumstances; for this is the will of God in Christ
Jesus for you!"

> "Day by day,
> Dear Lord, to Thee three things I pray:

o see Thee more clearly,
Love Thee more dearly,
Follow Thee more nearly,
Day by day." [9]

—RICHARD OF CHICHESTER

I yield myself anew into thy hands, O my God. I exist because of thee and without thee I would not exist. My smallest needs are of concern to thee as my largest. Therefore I turn myself again into thy hands—this clay with the life thou hast put in it. Turn and turn again my life. Give it thy form. When it is lacking in the best, break it again. I am thine. I have nothing to say. It is enough for me to serve thy grand design, and to keep nothing back from thy good pleasure which in the deepest sense is also mine. For this I was made.

Therefore ask, order, forbid. This is the purpose of my asking and knocking: what wouldst thou that I should do? What wouldst thou that I should not do? Raised, abased, comforted, suffering, intent upon thy works, I shall always adore thee, offering my will to thine. But to do so is no sacrifice. How could it be when I receive life and peace and victory as a result? I can only say in all things as Mary said, "Be it unto me according to thy word " [10]

V. INTERCESSION

1. I PRAY FOR OTHERS BECAUSE
I LOVE THEM AND GOD LOVES THEM

Intercessory prayer has become a great stumbling block to an adequate faith for modern man. His mind is set to think in terms of scientific cause and effect. Instead of praying for relief from polio, he believes in discovering and using a vaccine that immunizes a community from this dread disease. Instead of praying for the well-being of a loved one, he is more likely to expect help directly from his own efforts or through the efforts of others whom he may influence. Why, therefore, should he pray for others and what good will it do? These questions deserve an honest answer. We cannot keep our religious faith separated from our intelligent understanding of the world and of science. In these three sections on intercession let us look at our existence in a truly scientific way; that is let us examine all the facts and then act upon the highest convictions we can find. Only then can we know the meaning and value of prayer.

We pray for others because we love them and therefore cannot help but pray for them. We are bound together in a family, not only by blood ties, but by a common dependence on each other. "No man is an Iland, intire of itselfe." [1] Each of us is part of the mainland. Anything that happens to others happens to us, whether it be good or bad. Social scientists are emphasizing the truth that mankind is not a collection of individualistic atoms, but at our deepest levels we are united with all others. We are involved in each other whether we want to be or not.

It is most natural, therefore, not only for those who believe in prayer, but also even for skeptics, when loved ones are in great need, to lift up their hearts "to whatever powers there be!" Relic of superstition? Or sense of deepest reality? We need to know.

"I never believed in prayer," a big, self-sufficient man said to me, "but my son was ill. I was helpless. I prayed for the first time, 'God, whoever you are, whatever you are, have mercy on my little boy!' "

For those of us who believe in a loving Father God whose will is our highest good, it is even more natural that we should pray for those we love! We are all related to each other in God. We interpret the realities of our universe in terms of the Spirit of our Lord Jesus Christ.

A soldier wounded seriously at Salerno during World War II was recuperating in a convalescent section of Walter Reed Hospital in Washington. Every day he rode the streetcar five miles to Gray Stone Chapel and there joined with other soldiers in prayer for the cessation of the war and for peace. Why? Was it mere superstition? Was it an expression of a realistic faith? His answer is difficult to criticize: "I was out there with them. The least I can do for them now is to pray for them."

Could it be that we are closer together when we pray for each other than in any other moment and that geographical distance is less important than we think? If so, then the most, not the least, this soldier might do for his buddies would be to pray for them. The new physics of today rejects the old idea that every physical object is separate and isolated from all others in space. It teaches rather that each object is itself a field of force, a combination of millions of atoms filled with indescribable forces, but all related to each other. Every object from a stone to a star is a field of force related to larger and larger fields of force within the universe. There are no isolated particles of matter. Every particle of matter is alive with energy and is related to every other particle throughout the vastness of space.

If this is true of physical objects, how much more true of persons with minds that seem to have what we call telepathic powers of communication beyond our present imagination. It is not necessary to attack or defend the conclusions of Dr. J. B. Rhine and his associates of Duke University to recognize that our human minds are not entirely separate from each other. How much stronger is this unity if we believe we are related to each other in the mind of God. Prayer for others does not make an arbitrary and unnatural connection between us as isolated individuals, but uses the channels our Maker has created.

An even greater reason for praying for others is our conviction that God loves them and us, and through our co-operation God can do for them what we cannot do by ourselves. Prayer is not simply mental telepathy by means of which, through strong concentration, I am able to influence others. Whatever our reactions to the psi phenomena, as the evidences for mental telepathy are called, it is sure that God waits for our human co-operation before some things can be accomplished.

No one questions the necessity of co-operating with God in the physical realm. We seek to understand the laws of God and fulfill them when we send a rocket with its human cargo in quest of a landing on the moon. We co-operate with the wisdom and power of God when we lift our skyscrapers to the sky or fly our jet planes faster than the speed of sound. We are reverent and open-minded in dealing with electricity or atomic fission, believing the power is there if we learn how to release it. It is a tragic loss to our human life that so many of us who clearly see that co-operation with God is necessary on the physical level so that surgery and medicines are helps to nature's life-bringing powers, yet are so blind to the need to co-operate with God on moral and spiritual levels. While we are in the jet and space age physically, we are still in the ox-cart age morally and spiritually.

Christian prayer is based on the firm conviction that this is a spiritual universe under the rule of the love of God. There is a Divine Spirit at the heart and center of it who is in living and vital relationship to us. The apostle Paul affirms a very beautiful thing when he says: "The Spirit helps us in our weakness; for we do not know how to pray as we ought, but the Spirit himself intercedes for us with sighs too deep for words." (Rom. 8:26.) If the Spirit himself intercedes for us—and prays for us—then certainly we should pray for each other.

William Law says in *Serious Call to a Devout and Holy Life:*

There is no principle of the heart that is more acceptable to God than an universal fervent love to all mankind, wishing and praying for their happiness, because there is no principle of the heart that makes us more like God, who is love and goodness itself, and created all beings for their enjoyment of happiness through their growth and development.

Rabbi Mikhail declares: "I join myself to all of Israel, to those who are more than I, that through them my thought may rise and to those who are less than I so that they may rise through my prayer."

We are blessed when we pray for others and we are poor and ineffective in our own lives when we do not. One of the characters in the Bible puts it strongly: "Far be it from me that I should sin against the Lord by ceasing to pray for you!" (I Sam. 12:23.) Prayer for each other is one of the ways in which God intends for us to help each other. We labor together to build a house, a city, a nation. We talk together, sing together, laugh together. We pray together, fulfilling the deepest laws of our being.

We should and will pray for our own immediate family and friends, but beyond them is the larger family of God, the Church, "The body of Christ," the "communion of the saints," as Christians have called it. In the New Testament record we find not only our Lord but his apostles saying over and over:

Without ceasing I mention you always in my prayers. . . . For this reason I bow my knees before the Father, from whom every family in heaven and on earth is named, that according to the riches of his glory he may grant you to be strengthened with might through his Spirit in the inner

81

man, and that Christ may dwell in your hearts through faith; that you, being rooted and grounded in love . . . may be filled with all the fullness of God.

—Rom. 1:9; Eph. 3:14-17, 19[2]

All of this indicates that without our prayer there is a broken circuit in God's loving purposes. Just as the electricity from the dynamo cannot illumine an incandescent bulb when the circuit is broken, so God has chosen not to bring the fullness of love and help to our loved ones as long as we are missing links in the circle of prayer. Prayer for others completes the circuit enabling God in his wisdom to do what he could not otherwise do. Why? Cannot God do everything? Yes, within the limits of his purpose. But because we are made to be free, he does not force his good gifts upon us, even in the physical realm. Many millions of years of human history passed before man learned to fly. Not because the ability was not his, but because he had to learn how to use his powers in co-operation with God. So we must love him and help others find his love or something is missing.

2. I PRAY FOR OTHERS BECAUSE IN SO DOING OTHERS ARE HELPED AND SO AM I

Through our prayers others are helped. Sometimes this help comes indirectly, that is without our conscious intention. C. F. Andrews in Christ and Prayer tells the story of his father's prayer in the family circle one evening after he had discovered his good friend, whom he had entrusted with the management of his property, had robbed him of all his estate. It was a crushing blow, one the family did not get over financially; but his father prayed so lovingly, so understandingly for the man that something happened in the heart and life of his little son. No doubt his father would have been surprised to have known the effect of his prayer on the son.

"That night my soul was born," wrote Andrews. Though he does not tell us what happened to the faithless friend, we have good reason to hope that the loving prayers of one whom he had so wronged likewise had a powerful effect on him! But whether or no, the loving prayer of his father did have an effect on his own family.

"This I can well understand," the reader may be saying, "but what evidence do we have that intercessory prayer has a direct effect on the ones for whom we pray?" Much, indeed. There are numerous testimonies to the changes in spirit and character that have resulted from the prayer of others. How many persons are there whose mother or father or husband or wife or friend has prayed them into spiritual rebirth!

I, for one, must give my witness to the fact, though I I did not know it at the time, that my mother spent some time everyday lifting me up in prayer before the Lord and her prayers had a powerful influence on me. I am confident that as a youth many of my decisions—my choice of a way of life, my vocation, and my morals—could only be explained as the influence of her prayers.

You may say, of course, that it was not her prayers so much as her life. I answer that you cannot separate her prayers or anyone's prayers from their lives. Of one thing

I am sure: *I was included in the gracious triangle of my mother and her Heavenly Father. She loved me in God,* and this is the best description of intercessory prayer I know. She could have given me no gift more precious.

Through the years of my ministry I have known several strong, Christlike wives and husbands who have loved their marriage partners in the Lord. Though one was an alcoholic, a philanderer, a gambler or a materialist, the prayers of the companion were so effective that the other was not lost to his or her best self or to the home, though the chances were that just this would have happened!

One of these, I recall, prayed for her husband for ten years before seeing any change. During this time I counseled with her by letter and in person. Many of her communications with me revealed her struggles: to quit praying and loving and to give him up, or to use prayer as a magical force to make him do what she wanted. Then she came to the prayer of loving surrender to God and over a period of months found her prayers answered. She knew in advance that this does not always and necessarily take place. If it did, the freedom of the one prayed for would be removed. In her case the desired and longed for results did come, but whether or not it came she prayed in complete and loving surrender of him to God.

Of course her prayer had much to do with her own right attitude. You can't pray in Christlike love for another without changing your attitude toward him. It is surely accurate to say that holding him in the loving triangle of her relationship with God had a strong effect.

"Granted that faithful, loving intercession for others can provide spiritual help for others," you ask, "but how about the prayers in which physical help is sought, such as prayers for the recovery of health?" There are many illustrations of this kind of praying where physical help seems to come—so many in fact that while we may not be able to explain them in detail, we certainly cannot leave them out of any discussion of prayer. At the very least we can safely say that in such cases, spiritual victory is often realized regardless of the physical outcome.

As one out of many illustrations possible there is the account *After Everest* by Dr. Howard Somervell, Fellow of the Royal College of Surgeons and member of the Mt. Everest Expedition in 1922. He tells of a schoolmaster who had tuberculosis of the bone which the doctors reckoned had reached an almost incurable stage. They recommended immediate amputation of his leg to save his life. Dr. Somervell sent the X ray and diagnosis to India's greatest authority on bone disease who answered that the diagnosis was correct. The schoolteacher, being a man of faith, asked for three weeks: "I want to try the effect of praying about it." He left feverish, ill, and was carried by others. In three weeks he returned wonderfully improved to the amazement of the doctors. He told them that he had before him a life of service to God if only he could keep his leg and his life. He had called his family and friends together and asked them to unite in prayer for him and his leg. They agreed and for one week kept a continuous chain of prayer. Now he returned almost well and a few months later was back at school, "perfectly fit, playing games with the boys."

Whatever our faith or lack of faith about the connection between prayer and physical healing, the truth is this schoolmaster won a spiritual victory through his prayer and the prayers of others that would have been his even if he had not been restored to physical health. Who is to say that the one is not related to the other? At least we may agree that physical healing without spiritual health would have been useless and in the end valueless. This story declares a truth which our best intelligence cannot deny, however it is explained: "A good man's prayer is powerful and effective" (Jas. 5:16 N.E.B.).

We pray for others, for in so doing we are changed ourselves in significant ways. Our own attitudes are made more Christlike. Hostilities are removed. Guilt taken away. Our own willingness to help and wisdom concerning the best ways to lend our aid are increased.

William Law describes the wonderful change in the character of a man named Susurrus, who with all his religiosity and morality had one bad fault. He was an inveterate gossip and was inclined to dig up and pass on every choice morsel of the sins of others he could find, but always in a tender, compassionate manner. One day he was rebuked by a friend who told him to go home and pray for the one about whom he was gossiping. Susurrus was deeply hurt by the rebuke, but did as was suggested. William Law pictures the remarkable effect on Susurrus:

His heart is so entirely changed by it, that he can now no more privately whisper anything to the prejudice of another than he can openly pray to God to do people hurt.

Whisperings and evil-speakings now hurt his ears like oaths and curses: and he has appointed one day in the week to be a day of penance as long as he lives, to humble himself before God, in the sorrowful confession of his former guilt.[3]

> Lord, what a change within us one short hour
> Spent in Thy presence will prevail to make! [4]

One of the great saints of the Middle Ages was Angela of Foligno. When she first started to pray, it was an exceedingly selfish prayer. She hated her mother, her husband, and her children, wanted them to die, and prayed for it. But the more she prayed, the more she was changed. Her sense of fellowship with others including her family was enriched. Her hostilities were removed until now she sought the welfare of her worst enemies. "Therefore was I very ready to pray for them who did me evil, to love them with a very great love and to take compassion upon them."

"Pray for them which despitefully use you, and persecute you." said Jesus. "Rejoice, and be exceeding glad." (K.J.V.) Why? One of the reasons is that when you do you will be changed. You will still see their bad acts realistically and you will not like them any more then you did before but underneath the evil you will see them with all their sickness and need and love them. Whether or not they are changed, you will be.

We pray for others because in so doing the situation in which we and they live is changed. The fog is lifted so that they and we can see clearer and act more wisely. A circuit of love and trust in God is completed. God is able to do in and through them and for them as well as for us what he could not have done without destroying their freedom.

> More things are wrought by prayer
> Than this world dreams of.

. . . .

For so the whole round earth is every way
Bound by gold chains about the feet of God.[5]
—ALFRED L. TENNYSON

Since the Spirit prays for us and for those about us
with sighs too deep for words, let us also pray for others
and help complete the circuit!

3. WHAT GOD DOES WHEN WE PRAY
FOR OTHERS

We are here dealing with one of the most perplexing
but necessary questions connected with prayer for others.
"I can see how praying for others may help me to change
my attitudes toward them and be more willing and able
to help them. And if they know about my prayers for
them, they may be encouraged and influenced by the
knowledge of my care. But what I can't see is what God
does when I pray for others. Why would my praying
make any difference?"

This way of thinking is justified if you accept either
of two false views of God's action in our human life:

The first is represented by the Tyrolese peasant woman
described by Friedrich Heiler who "prayed incessantly
before a picture of Christ until she succeeded in bringing
our Lord into compliance with her wish and her husband
recovered his health. She was quite proud of her forceful
prayer." And we may surmise her husband may have
regretted her success! This approach, as we have said
before, ruins any prayer; for prayer that seeks to beg or

persuade God to change his mind is what the old Romans called "wearing out the gods." If your belief in prayer will rise or fall with your success in getting what you want, you will end up with no faith in prayer at all.

The other false view goes to the other extreme to think that God, "whoever or whatever he is," is shut up in a world of cold, impersonal laws which move on their implacable course, prayer or no prayer. To pray God to change his laws would be the height of superstition which no intelligent person would be guilty of doing. God isn't going to change his laws, hence there is no use for us to pray him to do so.

Either way, of course, you soon quit praying altogether, as millions have done. Certainly if prayer is no more than autosuggestion, you will soon quit praying if you ever begin. As James Bissett Pratt says so well: "If the subjective value of prayer be all the value it has, we wise psychologists of religion had best keep the fact to ourselves; otherwise the game will soon be up and we shall have no religion left to psychologize about." [6]

On the other hand, if you think God can be moved by your prayer to change his mind, you too will sometime quit praying when you fail to get him to do so.

Mark Twain's Huckleberry Finn describes how he tried prayer and gave it up as useless:

Miss Watson she took me in the closet and prayed, but nothing came of it. She told me to pray every day, and whatever I asked for I would get it. But it warn't so. I tried it. Once I got a fishline, but no hooks. It warn't any good to me without the hooks. I tried for the hooks three or four times, but somehow I couldn't make it work. By and by, one day, I asked Miss Watson to try for me, but she said I was a fool. She never told me why, and I couldn't make it out no way. I set down one time back in the woods, and had a long think about it. I says to myself, if a body can get anything they pray for, why don't Deacon Winn get back the money he lost on pork? Why can't the widow get back her silver snuffbox that was stole? Why can't Miss Watson fat up? No, says I to myself, there ain't nothin' to it.

This ridiculous illustration is no more ridiculous than the reasons many assign for having quit praying for themselves and others.

How different when we pray to God as Jesus revealed him, the almighty Creator Father, a personal Spirit whose highest purpose (laws or modes of acting) includes our relationship with him and our brothers. One of these deepest laws is that God cannot do his greatest good for us and others unless we pray. This principle is true in all personal relationships. How can I give the best gifts of my counsel and help to my daughters unless they love me and trust me enough to ask for my help. So God made us all free and will not force us against our wills.

Prayer therefore is not to change God's intention but to change God's action in fulfilling his intention. He has limited himself by giving us our freedom. *He loves those for whom we pray more than we do!* Never forget that when you pray desperately for a friend or loved one. God is more eager to help them than we are. He waits for us to co-operate with him through the use of doctors and other means and supremely through prayer. Let me illustrate.

Here is a wife praying for her husband who is an alcoholic or an immature philanderer. She may feel the whole burden on her shoulder, "God, please help"; but the weight is still on her and the problem is not changed. But she discovers the God of Christ whose grace is greater than she can imagine, and the burden is lifted; for now the greater part of it is on the shoulders of God. Her prayer is co-operation with the love of God! And when it is, things do begin to change.

Or here is a distraught mother praying for her dangerously sick child. She too may keep the burden on her shoulder if she chooses, as if she had to persuade God that he ought to do something to save her child! And then if the child does not get well, she may feel the Lord is her enemy, having failed to answer her prayer! How different the situation if she knows the burden is already on God's shoulders. He is more concerned than she to save the child. "It is not the will of my Father who is in heaven that one of these little ones should perish," said Jesus. But God in giving us freedom has chosen to wait for human co-operation: doctors, nurses, mother, father, friends, medicine, surgery, and prayer! When prayer is added to these other acts of co-operation or vice versa, God never fails to act. The child still may die as far as earthly existence goes, but the sting of bitterness and distrust are removed. As happens so often, however, when we co-operate with God in prayer and in all other things we know how to do, creative and health-bringing forces are released far greater than we know. For "in him we live and move and have our being." As individuals we have our roots in the heart of the Divine Love and when we pray in loving trust God always answers in the best way possible under the circumstances.

Here again is a secretary in an office, persecuted by an immature co-worker who makes her life miserable by trying to discredit everything she does and make her appear inefficient. Whether this is out of jealousy or competition is beside the point. Is the burden on this persecuted secretary's shoulders as she tried to pray about it or is it God's? What a difference in the way she prays if the latter. Then she is not trying to persuade God to "make Mary behave" or "get her out of my hair"; but she prays to co-operate with God to help Mary grow.

Our prayer when it is at its best restores and strengthens the relationship between us and God and in some indescribable way between God and the ones we pray for. We accept the miracle of radio and TV receiving sets which fulfill the conditions so that words and music and happenings in one place are sent to all parts of the world. Surely on the higher level of spiritual realities, the mind and heart of a loving God has provided for us channels of co-operation which, when used, may bring to us and our human loved ones the presence of a new and greater life than we yet know.

Leslie Weatherhead wrote of a member of City Temple facing a great ordeal:

It was not as though God could not help her without us, but he himself has ordained in a thousand situations that he desires to work with us. He would pick up our caring and turn it into her courage, our love and turn it into her will to get well, our solicitude and turn it into her serenity. God uses our caring to express his own.[7]

So God forbid that we should sin against his love by failing to pray for others.

> God uses us to help each other so,
> Lending our minds out.[8]
> —ROBERT BROWNING

Let us lend our minds and hearts and loves to God that we may help and strengthen each other!

4. HOW SHALL I PRAY FOR OTHERS?

We believe in God's steadfast love for us and those for whom we pray; therefore we pray for them in order to co-operate with God in doing the good for them and us which is infinitely better than we would do even at our best. Thus we may summarize our faith in intercessory prayer. By praying for them we are fulfilling one of the deepest of all God's laws. Relationships are set up through which healing and help flows.

Since this is so grandly true, how then should we pray for others? The answer of Christian experience is unequivocal—in the very same way we pray for ourselves: (a) with surrender of ourselves and of those for whom we pray to the goodness and love of God; (b) with an unfaltering trust in God's action and in our own efforts working with him.

First, there must be a surrendered life and will on my part. In acknowledgment that God's loving will is infinitely wiser than my own, I surrender my life and my will in trust to him. This is to say that the Christian life is a committed life, "from God through God and to God." Prayer is essentially adoration of God and self-giving to God, and in this self-giving we ask God for whatever we and our loved ones and neighbors need.

The question is: Do I commit my life and needs to him? Unless this happens my prayer is valueless. Alexander Whyte the great Scotch preacher tells of the time when a dear friend of his was very ill and near death. Whyte prayed for his friend that he might be spared to his family and his great work. One night as he prayed a voice seemed to speak to him: "Are you in real earnest in what you ask? Or are you uttering, as usual, so many of your idle words in this solemn matter?" The voice demanded that he give as "a solid proof that you are in real earnest" his consent to transfer to his sick friend "the half of your remaining years. Suppose you have two more years to live and work yourself, will you give over one of them to your friend? Or if you have ten years yet before you, will you let your friend have five of them?" "I sprang to my feet in a torrent of sweat," said Whyte. "It was a kind of Garden of Gethsemane to me. But, like Gethsemane, I got strength to say, 'Let it be as Thou hast said. Thy will be done. Not my will but Thine be done!'" That night Alexander Whyte lay down with a clean heart and a good conscience toward both God and his dear friend. He knew that his prayer that linked his love for his friend with God was right. "How the matter is to end I know not. . . . Enough for me and enough for you that my story is true and is no idle tale." [9]

The first requirement for effective prayer is a surrendered life and will on my part. Certainly I should be as vehement and strong in expressing my need and my longing for others as I feel it. Martin Luther's prayers were always vehement in the beginning, but not in the end. When he was being threatened with imprisonment and death before the Diet of Worms, he prayed passionately and urgently for his captors and for his own ability to come through with victory, but his prayer always ended with self-surrender: "Should my body perish for this cause, should it fall to the ground, yea, be broken to fragments, yet thy word and thy spirit are enough." At one time he prayed almost angrily for one of the electors who had fallen ill. Johannsen was important to his defense. Why should God let him be sick at such at time? Yet he concluded in calm commitment of it all to God: "O Lord, we are thine, do with us as thou wilt, only give us patience."

Our difficulty is that we are too often like the man who prayed, "Use me, Lord, but remember I always prefer to be used in an advisory capacity." No prayer with attached reservations is worth the time it takes.

The prayer of intercession requires an apostolic faith and love. When John Wesley was being threatened by the mobs with stoning and death, he prayed for them and for the people to whom he would preach. After praying he returned again and again to the places of danger. Obviously his prayers of intercession were always concluded in the spirit of this prayer of self-surrender which he placed at the climax of his Order for Watch-Night or New Year's Service:

I am no longer my own, but thine. Put me to what thou wilt, rank me with whom thou wilt; put me to doing, put me to suffering; let me be employed for thee or laid aside for thee, exalted for thee or brought low for thee; let me be full, let me be empty; let me have all things, let me have nothing; I freely and heartily yield all things to thy pleasure and disposal.

And now, O glorious and blessed God, Father, Son and Holy Spirit, thou art mine, and I am thine. So be it. And the covenant which I have made on earth, let it be ratified in heaven. Amen.[10]

So with Blaisé Pascal, strong-minded, stubborn-willed philosopher, scientist, Christian layman. During his long illness as he prayed for healing, he ended his prayer with this great surrender of trust: "Thou art Lord of all: do what thou wilt. Grant me, take from me, but make my will conform to thine, that being sick as I am, I may glorify thee in my sufferings!" This is the spirit of Christ-like prayer that enables God to act in us and others!

The key is not only surrender of our lives but trust in the action of God as we give ourselves to work with him. If we sincerely commit our lives and the lives of the ones for whom we pray in this attitude of complete trust, then we will pray for them *"not by asking, but by giving!"*

Dr. Glenn Clark made this secret of effective prayer clear in speaking with a mother who told him her son had infantile paralysis and the doctors had given him no hope to live. "Is there anything I can do?" she asked. He answered that she could certainly pray for him.

"How shall I pray?" she asked in obvious confusion.

"Pray, not by asking, but by giving," he answered. "As you ask you shall receive, but as you give you shall also receive; and the process of giving at a crisis like this will open your soul more completely than the process of asking. . . . As you give wholly, wholeness will come to you and to those that belong to you. But to give wholly is harder than it may seem. It means that you must give your boy completely and utterly to God. Let God take him into heaven [if necessary under the conditions of our human frailty]." . . .

"But I want my boy!" Dr. Clark answered that to want her son to lose the opportunity of fulfilling the great destiny God had for him would be mere "attachment" not according to the best plan for the boy [under the circumstances].[11]

This mother did give her son "with radiant acquiescence" to the Father. Within two months he was back in school without any trace of the polio. But if under the circumstances of our human frailty and the inadequacy of our ability to co-operate in dealing with polio the boy had died, his mother would still have trusted him to the Father.

In conclusion here are three steps to take in praying for others:

Wait in the presence of the glory and majesty and greatness of God in Christ until you are able to surrender to him in complete trust your life and the life of the one for whom you are praying.

Be willing to give yourself, a part of your own life if

necessary, in order to help the one for whom you are praying. Your love must be genuinely united with the love of God before your prayer is effective.

Give the one for whom you pray to God. Take your hands off. Think of placing his body, his problem, in the hands of the One whose loving mercy and wisdom are unsearchable and whose power and resources are inexhaustible!

My times are in Thy hand:
    My God, I wish them there;
My life, my friends, [my dear ones,] my soul,
    I leave entirely to Thy care.

My times are in Thy hand;
    Why should I doubt or fear?
My Father's hand will never cause
    His child a needless tear.

My times are in Thy hand;
    I'll always trust in Thee;
And after death, at Thy right hand
    I shall forever be.

—WILLIAM F. LLOYD

VI. TRUST

1. I AM ALWAYS ADEQUATE
"IN THE HOLLOW OF GOD'S PALM"

At the heart of the cyclone tearing the sky
And flinging the clouds and the towers by,
Is a spot of central calm;
So here in this roar of mortal things,
I have a place where my spirit sings,
In the hollow of God's palm.[1]

These beautiful words of Edwin Markham underline the final supreme element of effective, Christian prayer. Once we are willing to do God's will and have presented him our deepest needs, including the needs of others for whom we pray, then we need to trust in him. This is the heart of praying well.

The major result of trust is a deep, calm serenity which all the storms cannot shake. For the nature of a storm, physical or spiritual, is this: at its center is a place where the wind is calm. All around it are violent winds uprooting trees and houses. If one could stay in this central spot of calm, he would be safe. The analogy is not perfect, of course, for the eye of a hurricane moves rapidly, and it would be difficult to remain for long within the calm center of a storm. Even so, each storm brings with it stories of persons, animals, or houses that were in the center of the storm and came through unhurt.

So as human beings we may live at peace in the middle of a storm—the winds of hot words, angry complaints, bitter accusations, violent pressures. If we know how to pray the prayer of trust, we will have a place where our spirit sings, "in the hollow of God's palm."

Quite a picture, "in the hollow of God's palm!" Can you imagine it: a great hand and a little man in the hollow of it. Some of you recall the picture of Tom Thumb, based on the beloved nursery story. A little boy no larger than your thumb is helped by a kindly marketman who held him in the hollow of his hand. Of course this is a figure of speech. But all speech about God must use a symbol, and surely a symbol taken from personal life is better than one taken from mechanics!

You and I, whether we recognize it or not, are literally in God's palm. "In him we live and move and have our being." Every breath, every act, every thought is within the limits of God's wise and loving will. You cannot stretch out your arm without God. His wisdom and power make everything possible in our universe. The power in every atom, in every ray of light is God's power. As Christians we believe the power in and through all things is the power of the Divine Love, a love that is strong and wise, setting us free to work together with him for life and peace, or if we choose to refuse to cooperate, with resulting conflict and destruction.

Two things we can do "in the hollow of God's palm": First, we can leap out of God's palm. We may commit suicide all at once or little by little. When [...] laws of health, of spiritual and mental wel[...] we hate instead of love and are anxious [...] self-centered idolatry instead of confident in the fulfillment of our true mission in life—we commit suicide little by little. How many of us lose life "in a thousand small uncaring ways."

We may continue to live, but rebelliously, indifferently, halfheartedly, fighting ourselves, fighting others, fighting God. Anytime you are torn with fear, self-consciousness, hurt feelings you are rebelling at life and the God of life. This is our sin: not that we are finite, imperfect, mortal, and fragile; but that we are unwilling to accept ourselves in our human situation and make the best of it. We are defying the Spirit of love who created us, because of our lack of trust.

The other way to live is to trust ourselves and our fellows in the hollow of God's palm—what Jean Pierre de Caussade calls *Abandonment* [or *Absolute Surrender*] *to Divine Providence.* We are, he says, to "make a sacrament of the present moment," believing that whatever happens in the present moment God either sends with provident love or permits with the same wise love. He permits me to suffer when I do wrong to teach me the costly but priceless truth that can lead to new life. He permits the storms of weakness, pain, and finitude to whirl around me to teach me to trust in him rather than in my own strength. He permits others to hurt me and other innocent persons rather than to remove their freedom. He permits pains and sufferings which have no visible purpose. Since he permits these things, he expects

...e to seek and find the good in them that he is seeking to give me each moment and accept it.

This willingness to make a sacrament of the present moment is the deepest secret of effective prayer which can be better illustrated in life than in words. Let me give two stories with this in mind:

The first is the story of Captain George Barendese whose steamer Statendham was sunk by a German torpedo. His wife and children had been killed during the bombing by the Nazis. While in New York one Sunday in May, 1940, he visited with a minister friend after church. During the service he had sung with tears of strong faith in his eyes the great hymn "A Mighty Fortress is Our God." As he sat with the minister and his family at dinner he prayed this courageous prayer which is a tremendous illustration of what Caussade meant by making a sacrament of the present movement:

God help me not to hate, . . . give your guidance in thought, in speech and action to those who rule over the countries in war and . . . may your will be done and . . . your kingdom come. . . . God watch over my wife and boy. Before my wife was mine she belonged to you, Lord; before my little boy came to me he was yours, Father. They are in your hands. I trust you. May your will be done.[2]

He did not mean that it was God's will that the Nazis should have killed his wife and son and destroyed his ship. He meant that God's will was for him to accept these difficult facts and through the prayer of trust to find the way to inner peace and Christlike love in the moment of existence in which he found himself. The difference trust makes is all the difference between hope and despair, between victory and defeat, no matter what comes. It is the precious ability to put our lives into the channel of God's purposes to be flooded with his love and to act in harmony with his mighty will. This kind of trust comes from faith in God through Christ that says with the apostle Paul:

The Spirit himself endorses our inward conviction that we really are the children of God. Think what that means. If we are his children we share his treasures, and all that Christ claims as his will belong to all of us as well! Yes, if we share his sufferings we shall certainly share in his glory.

In my opinion whatever we may have to go through now is less than nothing compared with the magnificent future God has planned for us. The whole creation is on tiptoe to see the wonderful sight of the sons of God coming into their own. . . .

Moreover we know that to those who love God, who are called according to his plan, everything that happens fits into a pattern for good.

—Rom. 8:15-19, 28 Phillips

There is no more wonderful sight than that of "the sons of God coming into their own" through the prayer of trust! No wonder "the whole creation is on tip toe!"

The second story is one told by Dr. Daniel Poling of the time his son stood in his study before leaving for overseas service as a chaplain during the war. After a long silence he said: "Dad, I don't want you to pray for my return—that wouldn't be fair. Many will not return, and to ask God for special family favors just wouldn't be fair! . . . Pray, Dad, that I shall never be a coward. Pray that I shall have strength and courage and understanding of men, and especially that I shall be patient. Oh, Dad, just pray that I shall be adequate!" [3]

This prayer was answered as all will agree who know the story of Clark Poling and how he and three other chaplains went down with their ship in the Atlantic. The war was not God's will, nor the loss of so many wonderful lives; but this young man's prayer for himself and the prayer of his dad ("pray that I may be adequate") was certainly fulfilled. The prayer of trust includes the worst "what-if's"; it takes the fear and desperation out and makes us adequate in the sunshine and the shadow!

No wonder the church fathers in saying our Lord's prayer added the magnificent conclusion, "For thine is the kingdom, and the power, and the glory" (K.J.V). There is no other way to end a prayer in the name of Christ than in a great affirmation of trust.

"Thine is the kingdom," Lord. I am part of it. So is all this universe with its dependable laws and its mysterious powers. Your will is my perfect freedom. Even if I cannot understand all the "why," I trust your rule.

"Thine is the power," Lord. All the strength and help I need to meet this moment and the next is available to me. I can do all things through thee who gives me power!

"Thine is the glory," Lord. All the joy and peace I need in this moment—the glory of life—is here for the taking. Only the prayer of trust can see and accept it. I do now trust you in this moment and for all that is to come!

2. THE KINGDOM OF GOD HAS COME NEAR ME

Jesus was sending out the seventy, two by two, ahead of him into the villages and towns to prepare the way for his coming. They were to say to the people, "The kingdom of God has come near to you." This was to be their message. (Luke 9.)

In this short space it is impossible to discuss all that Jesus meant by "the kingdom of God" (or "the kingdom of heaven," "life in abundance," "eternal life," or "salvation"—phrases which the New Testament uses almost interchangeably). He meant at least this much: the rule or reign of God is over all his universe, including our human life. To be "in the kingdom of heaven" is to accept joyfully and thankfully the new relationship of love and trust with God so gloriously seen in his own life. To be able to know and to do his good will, to act with wisdom, courage, and love, so that even though you are hungry, poor, in mourning, or persecuted, you possess a blessedness and victory which the world can never give nor take away—this is to be in the kingdom of heaven, to possess eternal Life. The Beatitudes are the best description of the life of anyone who is living in God's heavenly kingdom. (See Matt. 5:1-12.)

We are indeed next door to heaven! But we may not recognize it. We may rebel at the requirements of the kingdom, disobey its laws, neglect or refuse the relationships for which we are made, and thus lose our way in life, and find not heaven but hell, even now. We cannot evade or avoid the kingdom of God any more than we can live without air and food and water. Either we live in it with glad awareness of its Lord and thankful acceptance of his resources, or we meet it in continued judgment with growing discord, meaninglessness, and frustration. "You are not far from the kingdom of God," said Jesus to the scribe who came asking what is the greatest law of God.

How do you get in this kingdom, stay in it, live in it? Not through your righteous acts and good deeds, not through any number of good forms or orthodox beliefs, not even through any number of hours and days of prayer. (See Matt. 7:21-28; I Cor. 13; Gal. 5:22.) These should come and will be valuable as fruits of the kingdom, but you cannot make yourself a part of God's kingdom by practicing virtue, obeying the law, and doing good.

You enter the kingdom by faith: a commitment of your life to the rule of God and trusting him who is always near to guide, strengthen, and help you. "Fear not, little flock," said Jesus, "for it is your Father's good pleasure to give you the kingdom."

Even though we were dead in our sins God, who is rich in mercy, because of the great love he had for us, gave us life together with Christ—it is, remember, by grace and not by achievement that you are saved—and has lifted us right out of the old life to take our place with him in Christ in the Heavens. . . . It was nothing you could or did achieve— it was God's gift to you.

—Eph. 2:5-8 Phillips

If the kingdom of God is so near, why are so many of us who profess to believe in God so far away? So prone

106

to lose our lives in anger, self-pity, fear, anxiety, envy, jealousy, greed, and selfishness?

Because the gift has not been received by us. We do not accept the kingdom for we are not primarily dedicated to the will of God and we simply do not trust the loving presence and help of God.

The only action that will fit us to receive his gift is the act of total trust. This is the creative deed which revolutionizes our communion with God. It is the heart and soul of the life of prayer. For the prayer which arises out of total trust is the prayer through which we accept and live in the kingdom that is here.

"For every one who asks receives, he who seeks finds, and to him who knocks it will be opened," said Jesus. Yes, but you do not keep knocking at a door that is already open and the host is inviting you to come in! You accept —you enter—you receive! "See, I stand knocking at the door. If anyone listens to my voice and opens the door, I will go into his house and dine with him, and he with me." (Rev. 3:20 Phillips.)

Holman Hunt has illustrated this great statement in his painting, "The Light of the World." Our Lord is seen knocking on the door of our human life with a lighted lantern in his hand and the latchstring is *inside*. It is we who must open:

> O Jesus, thou art standing
>   Outside the fast-closed door,
> In lowly patience waiting
>   To pass the threshold o'er.
> Shame on us, Christian brethren,

His Name and sign to bear,
O shame, thrice shame upon us,
To keep him standing there!

O Jesus, thou art knocking;
And lo, that hand is scarred,
And thorns thy brow encircle,
And tears thy face have marred.
O love that passeth knowledge,
So patiently to wait;
O sin that hath no equal,
So fast to close the gate!
—WILLIAM WALSHAM HOW

Yes, we are knocking but he is knocking also: the "Double Search" as Rufus Jones puts it. He sought and is seeking us before we seek him!

"The kingdom of God has come near you." God has been trying for centuries to tell us about the wonderful uses of electricity and atomic power. Only after Ben Franklin flew his kite and Oppenheimer, Compton, and their helpers made the first atomic reactor did man open the door to accept and realize this power.

The kingdom of love and peace, of hope, of joy and power for great and unselfish living has come near to you! *The prayer of trust opens wide the door!*

Here is a victim of a dread disease, fighting with fear, pain, and misery, and the fear is worse than the pain. The kingdom of God has come near him, but he cannot accept it; for his attention is on his fear, his loss, the suffering and death ahead. Then someone helps him to meet the Christlove at the heart of all things.

Through commitment and trust he too can say with the apostle Paul:

Christ died for us, Christ rose for us, Christ reigns in power for us, Christ prays for us!

Can anything separate us from the love of Christ? Can trouble, or pain or persecution? Can lack of clothes and food, danger to life and limb, the threat of force of arms? . . .

No, in all these things we win an overwhelming victory through him who has proved his love for us.

I have become absolutely convinced that neither death nor life, neither messenger of Heaven nor monarch of earth, neither what happens today nor what may happen tomorrow, neither a power from on high nor a power from below, nor anything else in God's whole world has any power to separate us from the love of God in Jesus Christ our Lord!
—Rom. 8:34-35, 37-39 Phillips

Suddenly by an act of faith this man opens his hands to accept the gift—his eyes to see it—his soul to believe it—and his prayers lift him into a world he never knew. He still has pain, but his deepest misery is gone. He lives in the kingdom during those months with increasing victory, so that his family and friends witness that these months were his most creative and blessed!

How oft I have seen it in my ministry: three months, six months, six years in the kingdom of God result in greater growth and achievement than all the years preceding!

Here is a youth imprisoned in self-conscious inadequacy. Feeling within himself powers greater than he has ever used, he is discouraged because obviously his parents do not believe in him—or at least they never pay much attention to him except to see that he has enough to eat and good clothes and a car. Inside he is so insecure and afraid. He may either put on a bold front, bluster and brag, and race his car and his life doing dangerous things to get attention—to be thought of as a "leader" of a gang; or he may just pull into his shell, burning up with resentment toward those who are able to be free and effective as he is not. Either way the harder he tries to be at his best, the more he is at his worst. He becomes either a juvenile delinquent or a solitary soul burning up with hell on the inside. We say to him, "The kingdom of God has come near to you." Heaven is at hand—but he laughs— "God?" God is the word he uses to "cuss" with, or it is the word which his parents use as a policeman to make him do what they want him to do. He has no use for this word.

Then something happens, an accident, some crisis; and a friend comes who puts in his hands a book telling the story of Albert Schweitzer. Or he discovers the New Testament translated in modern speech and confronts the life and spirit of Jesus. As he reads he begins to be conscious of this unseen kingdom that has surrounded him all these years without his ever knowing it. One day he pulls the latchstring, and the Christ spirit enters. He surrenders the "nots" that have been burning within him. He hears and answers a call to relieve the suffering of humanity as Jesus and Schweitzer did. He decides to accept and live in the kingdom, no matter the cost. He goes back to school and enters medical training; he forgets himself, loses his timidity or his braggadocio, puts his heart into his study, and becomes a great doctor whose remarkable powers of healing are in the realm of the spirit, even as much as in the physical realm. He is no longer next door to heaven; he is in it!

Or here is a tired mother and wife with four normal but irritating children and an equally normal but irritating husband. She is ill-tempered, sharp-tongued, a nag to both husband and children. She tries to improve herself, to stop nagging—she hates herself—but the harder she tries, the more bound up she becomes, and life is hell. Then she hears her minister say, "The kingdom of God has come near to you." At first it angers her: "How could it be, in my situation? He just doesn't know what I have to put up with." Then one day a friend, who is in just such a situation also, tells of her new victory. At last she quietly relinquishes her own children, her husband, her dread of getting older in God's hands. She begins to receive the calm strength and perspective that puts things in their proper order. Rising a few minutes earlier she "makes up her soul" every morning before she makes up her beds. She takes time now for thinking, reading, and meditation; she begins to live in this kingdom. More and more her trust makes her aware of the kingdom of abundant energy and love in which the hardest experiences are met with relative ease and life takes on new meaning. She begins to live purposefully, confidently, lovingly. She isn't an angel overnight, of course. She still loses her temper once in a while. But ask her children and her husband—they know better than anybody—the kingdom of heaven is near to them.

What is the kingdom of selfish hell in which you live?

A youth in self-conscious inadequacy, a parent with a sharp temper, a successful man with a deep anxiety or a deadening boredom and emptiness? Whatever it is and whoever you are, the kingdom of God has come near to you!

3. I FIND SALVATION IN SURRENDER

"Something we were withholding left us weak." The words were heard by a hundred-million Americans in a dramatic moment in our history. Robert Frost the beloved-old poet was reading his poem, "The Gift Outright," at the Inauguration of John F. Kennedy as President of the United States. The world situation was filled with potential dynamite. Our future as a nation and a world was uncertain. The people were tense. Before the new President gave his inaugural address Robert Frost arose to read words which will not likely be forgotten. Recalling the situation back in the time of the American Revolution he read:

> But we were England's, still colonials,
> Possessing what we still were unpossessed by,
>
> . . . .
>
> Something we were withholding left us weak
> Until we found out that it was ourselves
> We were withholding from our land of living
> And forthwith found salvation in surrender.
> Such as we were we gave ourselves outright
>
> . . . .
>
> To the land vaguely realizing westward,

But still unstoried, artless, unenhanced,
Such as she was, such as she will become.[4]

Robert Frost was declaring the mighty truth: we today or in any day can never find any salvation except through surrender. The truth extends far beyond the realm of citizenship. We must give ourselves outright not only to our country but to that which is eternally worth doing and being in God's kingdom. It is that something which we are withholding that makes us weak, spiritually or in any other way. That is until I give the best I have to the highest I know in complete trust I am not able to live in complete freedom and power to be at my best. The choicest gifts of God come to me only when I trust him enough to give myself outright to him and his purposes.

Health is a gift. I find the salvation of my health in surrender—the surrender of myself in sleep, in relaxed exercise, and in trustful living—the surrender of hurtful habits, poisonous beverages or foods or attitudes. When it comes to health the things I am withholding always leave me weak.

So in our homes, there is no salvation from the jealousies and bickerings that make us weak except through surrender. Home is a precious gift to that family whose members give themselves outright to each other. "Love seeketh not her own"; that is love does not demand her own rights. Something else is more important in a home which reflects the kingdom of heaven: not getting my way but finding the truly-good way for us all. We never really trust each other until we find salvation in surrender, not to each other's whims, for that would be chaos, but to the loving will of God for each and all.

There is no trust without surrender and without trust there is no genuine happiness. The one who says, "I must be happy," is always the one who is the most unhappy. It is only when we surrender and trust ourselves to the creative quest for the highest good as God gives it that we find happiness slipping up behind us and suddenly before we know it we are possessed by it.

Life is in surrender to God! This is the ultimate meaning of the prayer which ends in trust. "We are not here to work but to be worked upon," wrote Emerson. An ancient Egyptian saying declares, "The boatman reacheth the landing partly by pulling, partly by letting go. The archer shooteth the target partly by pulling, partly by letting go."

Prayer at its best is the surrender of our little, failing selves to him to be cleansed, renewed, strengthened, and led. Like the boatman and the archer we pray by pulling and pulling until we get our desires in line with his, but the time comes when our prayer is completed by letting go.

It is the greatest marvel of the Christian character, that the completest self-sacrifice gives the completest self-possession; that only the captive soul, which has flung her rights away, has all her powers free; and that simply to serve under the instant orders of the living God is the highest qualification for command. This is the meaning of the great saying of Cromwell's, "One never mounts so high as when one knows not whither one is going," a saying which "the wise and prudent" scorned as a confession of blindness, but which reveals to simpler minds the deepest truth.[5]

Recently I came into a hospital room where lay one who in the last weeks had met the ravages of a deadly malignancy with such winsome trust that her life was offering an exalted witness to the love of God which her easier days of health had never given. She had been given salvation from the bitterness and self-pity that would have left her weak. That salvation was hers by the surrender of her life in trust to God in whatever came. With all who visited her she shared her experience of joy and victory:

"I am not afraid to trust my body to the bed. It can hold me up. Why therefore should I not trust my life in the hands of my Heavenly Father?"

Because she withheld nothing, she was kept strong in spirit even to the last! It is impossible for those of us who witnessed her victory not to believe that even in death she found salvation in surrender!

It is always easier to surrender things or others than ourselves. One of my good friends who has had considerable growth in the meaning and use of Christian prayer wrote me recently:

I have had some amazing experiences in answered prayer with others. It is so thrilling and exciting to see how wonderfully God works things out when He is allowed to! It is so simple for me to release others' problems to Him in love and confidence and I can release mine—but I keep grabbing mine back! Poor God—how weary He must get of the constant snatching and giving back, snatching and giving back. It's a wonder He doesn't throw them in my face and finally say, "Oh, for Pete's sake, keep them and solve them yourself." Someday I'll learn!

This is our greatest trouble. Yes, even for mature Christians. We are always giving and then snatching back. But God is not going to give us up. His patience is from everlasting to everlasting but his love is strong enough to let us suffer the weakness that results from our continual snatching back. Some day we will learn!

My own experience contains countless times when I snatched back what once I had given and was weak thereby. And yet I know the joy and power of salvation in surrender.

Of this I am sure:

> When I withhold one thing, dear Lord, from Thee,
> Then I am weak and spent and cannot see
> The free, creative one I'm meant to be:
> Salvation is surrender, Lord, to Thee!
>
> I go to live and work without a sigh—
> I give myself outright to live and die
> For the dear realm of hope for all humankind.
> With joyful trust I serve with quiet mind.
>
> I gladly use what days or years remain;
> Thy glorious Kingdom's goal I yet shall gain!
> Salvation in surrender, Lord, to Thee!
> And in Thy blessed grace I shall be free!
>
> —LANCE WEBB

One of the most significant meanings of the prayer of surrender and trust comes to those who suffer as a result of committing themselves to what they believe is God's will in the cause of justice, helping people imprisoned by the prejudice and greed of evil systems. Surely they will receive the great peace and contentment described in Isaiah 53:11 as God's gift to his suffering servant: "He shall see the fruit of the travail of his soul and be satisfied."

It is easy to do God's will as we work with him for the right when the cause is popular. But when we must bear the cross of calumny, opposition, and injury, how easy to snatch back our commitment of trust! The only way our dedication to action in the Spirit of Christ can be lasting and effective is as we continue to give ourselves in trust and confidence for the invincible purposes of the loving, righteous Father God who rules the universe! The prayer of François Fénelon gives the best words I know to this prayer of trust:

Lord, I know not what I ought to ask of Thee; Thou only knowest what I need; Thou lovest me better than I know how to love myself. O Father; give to Thy child that which he himself knows not how to ask. I dare not ask either for crosses or consolations; I simply present myself before Thee. I open my heart to Thee. Behold my needs which I know not myself; see and do according to Thy tender mercy. Smite or heal; depress me, or raise me up; I adore all Thy purposes without knowing them; I am silent; I offer myself in sacrifice; I yield myself to thee; I would have no other desire than to accomplish Thy will. Teach me to pray. Pray Thyself in me. Amen.[6]

VII. RECOLLECTION

"All that you have said of the experience of prayer may be true," you may say with some heat, "but I have been unable to pray like this: to be honest and open in confessing the false shells that imprison me—to be glad in my commitment and dedication to God's will—to pray for what I need and for what others need with surrender and trust. I can understand how necessary all this is if I am to experience the peace and creative joy and victory of God in Christian prayer. But how do I get to the place where I can make such a surrender in trust?"

This question doubtless is the one that bothers all of us the most. It is one thing to know the conditions of prayer. It is another to be able to fullfill them. These last two sections are dedicated to the consideration of our inability to pray as we know we ought to pray and to suggestions of ways in which we may go about it more effectively.

1. I FIND MY "LISTENING POINT"

There are two things you and I need so very greatly: (a) We need someone to listen to us as we speak of our deepest longings and complaints; and (b) we need above everything else to be able to listen ourselves to One who can satisfy our deepest longings. These two needs are really one: for if I find a listening point where someone is able to listen to me, I may then be able to listen, and from this listening I find my desires changing so that they are one with God's. I receive the power to pray with genuine surrender and trust. Only then am I able really to listen to others.

Sigurd F. Olson, a naturalist and guide in the Lake Superior country in northern Minnesota, has written an absorbingly beautiful book in which he describes how after long search he found his *Listening Point*:

I had come through woods and swamps off the end of a road and was suddenly out of the brush and trees on an open shelf of rock. There it was as I had dreamed, a composite picture of all the places in the north I had known and loved. . . . Each time I have gone there I have found something new which has opened up great realms of thought and interest. For me it has been a point of discovery . . . from which I have seen the immensity of space and glimpsed at times the grandeur of creation. . . . For me it would be a listening post from which I might even hear the music of the spheres. . . . Everyone has a listening point somewhere. It does not have to be in the north or close to the wilderness but some place of quiet where the universe may be contemplated with awe.[1]

Where is the listening point from which you and I may look out on our lives and the life of the universe? Where we may find meaning and courage and power as we listen to God and the music of the spheres, and whisperings of his infinite truth and never-failing hope and eternal love so that our desires are changed and our wills transformed?

The finding of this place is what Christians have called practicing the presence of God in recollection and communion. We may have friends, family, counselors who listen to us occasionally, but none of them can supply this our deepest need. As Taylor Caldwell puts it in her inspiring story *The Man Who Listens:*

One of the terrible aspects of this world today is that nobody listens to anyone else. Not even those who love you and would die for you—your parents, your children, your friends, they have no time. If you are sick, or bewildered, or frightened, or lost or bereaved, or alone or lonely—nobody really listens. Even the clergy are hurried and harassed: they do their best and work endlessly. . . . Whose fault is it? I don't know, but nobody seems to have any time.[2]

The words are spoken by a retired lawyer, John Godfrey, as he explains to the press the reasons for leaving all his wealth to a foundation dedicated to the building and upkeep of a beautiful white marble chapel situated in the tastefully landscaped grounds in the center of a great city. Here people might come and tell their sorrows, complaints, and needs to "the Man Who Listens," and he would always have time, all the time needed. The book is a composite story of twelve souls who came to talk— and remained to listen. Among them were a rich society woman who despised her husband; a factory worker who felt he never had a chance; a Black who felt despised and forsaken because of his color and his bitter experiences; an aged mother who felt unwanted and unhonored by her children; a father whose only son, a brilliant doctor dedicated to cancer research, was dying with the dread disease; a minister who felt like a liar and a hypocrite because he was giving his people what they wanted rather than what he knew they needed; a famous architect whose life had no meaning; a discouraged teacher; a confused judge; and an atomic scientist who was in agony over what he should do with the discoveries that could mean life or destruction to the world.

Each one came, in spite of his cynicism and skepticism, to talk to the Man Who Listens. Each poured out his or her story in the little white room to the unseen man behind the curtain. Did he speak to them? They were not quite sure. But as they talked, a strange, new ability to give voice to their real questions about life and destiny was given, questions even those who had gone to a psychiatrist or a minister had never been able to ask before. At last in utter sorrow or anger or despair they touched the button, as the instructions directed, and the curtain flew open revealing the identity of the Man Who Listens.

In a huge alcove twelve feet wide and flooded with light hung a large crucifix of roughly carved wood on which was nailed a carved-ivory figure of the Christ, Son of God and Son of man—not dead, but living. His head with its crown of thorns was lifted and held forward "listening, suffering, yet hearing. The eager eyes were turned on [each one] listening." [3] And in his presence for the first time they too began to listen and to hear the truth they needed—to receive the hope and courage and love necessary for life and death! Here they found the ability to pray, "Thy will be done" not mine.

The book is a parable, of course—fiction, if you want

to call it that. And yet it is a true story of our human life. Each one in that room found, as each of us may, a listening point in the presence of the One Who Always Listens to us through all our cynicism, dejection, fear, hatred, complaining, self-pity, or despair. And we are able to listen for the first time and see the loving truth that brings meaning, courage, insight, strength, and life even in the midst of death. This is the experience of countless persons in every age. The heart of our Good News as Christians is that there is always One Who Listens to us. He it was who said, "And, when I am lifted up from the earth, will draw all men to myself." (See John 12:27-36.)

In the New Testament account of Mary and Martha and Jesus, Martha represents most of us: so busy, so rushed, so occupied with many things, too busy to listen. But "she had a sister called Mary, who sat at the Lord's feet and listened to his teaching." No doubt this was not the first chapter to her story. There was a time when she could not listen. She too had first to pour out her bitter story of guilt and doubt and discouragement before him. But he had listened and now she could listen. "One thing is needful," said Jesus. "Mary has chosen the good portion, which shall not be taken away from her." (See Luke 10:42-48.)

Our listening point is at his feet, whether it be a place in the wilderness of Minnesota or Canada or Columbus or Chicago. Nature itself has nothing to say to us except as we view it through his life and truth. When he is lifted up before us and we let him listen, we too can listen.

Read the Gospels and mark the times when he

listened: to the cry of the leper wanting to be healed; the complaint of the paralytic with his grumbling and guilt, bitter against God and man; the widow weeping for her son; the screams of the demented who like many of us had their minds filled with tormenting devils. First he listened to them—and something happened that led them to listen to him. In his presence they like us met the Mighty Love before whom we may pour out all our story and know that we are heard without condemnation (we have enough of that already), with no cheap advice (we have too much of that), and with no hurry but with time, all of the time we need.

Ministers, psychiatrists, counselors, and others have helped countless persons through the years by listening to them. But no one of us with our human limitations can ever approximate the divine ability of the Eternal Listener for three reasons: (a) the limit of our time, (b) the limit of our human strength, endurance, and patience, and (c) the emotional involvement with those who talk with us.

What we cannot do, our Lord does. As the prophet Isaiah describes the Eternal Suffering Servant:

> Surely he has borne our griefs
>   and carried our sorrows;

> .   .   .   .

> But he was wounded for our trans-
>   gressions,
>   he was bruised for our iniquities;

> .   .   .   .

and with his stripes we are
healed.

—Isa. 53:4-5

In his presence at the moment and the place where you have poured out your heart you may find your listening point. You may begin to hear the "still sad music of humanity," to find sympathy, understanding, and forgiveness for your loved ones and even for your enemies just as did those early Christians waiting at the foot of his cross. So have the streams of burdened, willful, stubborn souls through the years discovered the glorious-marching music of God's purposes and the call to come and work with him.

No matter what our sorrow or burden, he has carried it before us. Let us bow or kneel before him and pray:

> Master, speak! Thy servant heareth,
>   Waiting for Thy gracious word,
> Longing for Thy voice that cheereth;
>   Master! Let it now be heard.
> I am listening, Lord, for Thee:
> What hast Thou to say to me?
>   —Frances R. Havergal

2. "I KEEP THE LORD ALWAYS BEFORE ME"

The great secret of Christian prayer as it becomes a true listening point can be summed up in these words of the psalmist who lived long before Christ:

The Lord is my chosen portion and my cup.

. . . .

I keep the Lord always before me,
  because he is at my right hand,
    I shall not be moved.

—Ps. 16: 5, 8

The highest use of our freedom to think as we choose is what the saints call the regular habit of *recollection*. The apostle Paul was recommending this essential discipline of our minds when he wrote to the Thessalonians, "Rejoice always, pray constantly, give thanks in all circumstances; for this is the will of God in Christ Jesus for you."

Of course God is always before us and with us, but our trouble is in recognizing him. The act of recollection is the act of consciously recalling who we are and who God is: keeping the Lord always before us. Not that we are to think of God at every moment of the day. We couldn't get anything else done if we did that; but as often as possible. I must bring the presence of God into my conscious thought and at all other times I must attempt to live in the serene confidence of his presence.

One never gets to the listening point without consciously recollecting that the God of Christ is *here*, listening to us, waiting for us to listen to him. The power of prayer comes to one who by an act of faith repeated continuously day by day, many times a day, recollects himself in the Presence of listening love: Lord, you are with me, here and now! Thy spirit is within me! Thy love is waiting to hear, to heal, to strengthen, to lead!

All of this is to say that no one ever stumbles accidentally onto the great discoveries either in prayer or in science. Obviously the advances in science are the result of disciplined seeking—perhaps not for the exact truth discovered, but at least for truth. Every discovery in the present is made by recollecting the truths and experiences of the past and adding them to the present which we confront with a completely open and surrendered mind. Certainly all who have found the joy and power of prayer will testify to the necessity for such disciplined recollection. The witness of the saints from Paul to Thomas R. Kelly, the great-spirited Quaker, is unanimous in this respect. Listen to his classic statement in *The Testament of Devotion:*

How, then, shall we lay hold of that Life and Power, and live the life of prayer without ceasing? By quiet, persistent practice in turning of all our being, day and night, in prayer and inward worship and surrender, toward Him who calls in the deeps of our souls. Mental habits of inward orientation must be established. An inner, secret turning to God can be made fairly steady, after weeks and months and years of practice and lapses and failures and returns. . . . Begin now, as you read these words, as you sit in your chair, to offer your whole selves, utterly and in joyful abandon, in quiet, glad surrender to Him who is within. In secret ejaculations of praise, turn in humble wonder to the Light, faint though it may be. Keep contact with the outer world of sense and meanings. Here is no discipline of absent-mindedness. Walk and talk and work and laugh with your friends. But behind the scenes, keep up the life of simple prayer and inward worship. Keep it up throughout the day. Let inward prayer be your last act before you fall asleep and the first act when you awake. And in time you will find as did Brother Lawrence, that "those who have the gale of the Holy Spirit go forward even in sleep." [4]

At least two things are involved in keeping the Lord always before us in continued acts of recollection and communion: (a) looking to God and not to our feelings, and (b) looking to God and not to the demands of our self-image with its twisted desires.

Most of us are tempted to keep our feelings always before us. I had been trying to pray for several years before I discovered how fatal it is to identify a certain feeling with God's presence. As Screwtape, the Devil's chief assistant in C. S. Lewis' stimulating satire, said to one of the minor Devils as he coached him in his attempts to divert his young charges from real prayer:

The simplest [way of preventing them from doing so] is to turn their gaze away from Him towards themselves. Keep them watching their own minds and trying to produce feelings there by the action of their own wills. . . . When they meant to pray for courage, let them really be trying to feel brave. When they say they are praying for forgiveness, let them be trying to feel forgiven. Teach each of them to estimate the value of prayer by their success in producing the desired feelings.[5]

To keep our feelings uppermost as the test of God's presence is to be at the mercy of a dozen things that influence our emotions; such as how tired or rested we are, the state of our digestion, the time of the month, the state of our pocketbook, bank account, reputation, or success in our work. Thus if we depend on feelings the very times when we need to pray most we are the least likely to find the Presence who listens and restores us to the ability to hear and do the highest and best. The truth is, as Abbé de Tourville says, that we are

never so near God as when we have to get on as well as we can without the consolation of feeling his presence. Do not worry about your feelings, but act as if you had those which you would like to have. This is not done by making a mental effort, nor by seeking to feel that which you do not feel; but by simply doing without the feeling you have not got and behaving exactly as if you had it. When you realize that lack of feeling does not hinder reality, you will no longer put your trust in your [feelings].[6]

The important thing is to accept yourself in the Presence by faith and live and act with loving confidence. To keep the demands of our self-image uppermost, of course, is equally fatal. If when we recollect ourselves in his Presence, we insist on our way, our rights, our desires, we turn the act of prayer into an act of magic by which we seek to use the Almighty to our purposes. Recollection that leads to communion, therefore, must include a steady repetition of the surrender and trust which was made when we first began to pray by faith. The point is: this commitment is made not once but continuously. As often as I remember who I am and reaffirm my trust in his goodness and accept his love, I reaffirm my complete and unreserved surrender of myself to do his will. At each moment I say, in effect:

O Lord, I give all that I know of myself to all that I know of you, to be and to do all that in your glorious purpose I am meant to be and to do, as you shall reveal it to me and give me the power!

3. TIMES AND PLACES FOR RECOLLECTION

We have considered in previous chapters the necessity of a surrendered will. Here we need to share the experience of those who have learned the importance of times and places for recollection at which we confront God often and regularly enough so that we will be able to surrender ourselves to him.

It is not enough to wait until the crises. If we do, we may find our emotions so overwhelmed by fears and hostilities that we simply cannot meet God. The person who has consistently, weekly, daily for five, ten, twenty-five years set aside some time for this priceless act is the person who when the crisis comes is most likely to be able to listen and learn and receive from the Lord.

The story is told that during the early hours of the Battle of Gettysburg Abraham Lincoln was pacing up and down, lonely and troubled, as the battle reports came in and the fate of the Union was in the balance. Later on he described to his friends what he did. He went into his room, locked the door, knelt, and prayed something like this: "I told God that I had done all that I could and that now the result was in His hands; that if this country was to be saved it was because He so willed it! The burden rolled off my shoulders. My intense anxiety was relieved and in its place came a great trust-fulness." [7]

But this is not all of the story. For months and years preceding his crisis Lincoln had practiced recollection and communion with God regularly in the same whole-hearted surrender. No wonder he found strength that night.

> When I think of thee upon my bed,
>   and meditate on thee in the
>   watches of the night;
> for thou hast been my help,
>   and in the shadow of thy wings
>   I sing for joy.

Thus the writer of the sixty-third psalm describes a regular habit of recollection that brought help and joyous reality in prayer. Another ancient singer declares his experience of bitterness and temptation when:

> My feet had almost stumbled,
>   my steps had well nigh slipped.
>
> .   .   .   .
>
> until I went into the sanctuary of
>   God;
>
> .   .   .   .
>
> [Now] My flesh and my heart may fail,
>   but God is the strength of my
>   heart and my portion for ever.
>   —Ps. 73: 2, 17, 26

Let me tell you the story of one of the greatest Christian laymen of my acquaintance. He was the kind of man everyone in the Church instinctively thought of when you mentioned the word "Christian." His influence was great not only in his church but in the city. He had come through the depression, business failure, a serious illness, and the loss of his dear companion with a clearer and more victorious witness than ever. One day as I sat in his office I asked him to share with me, if he could, the one thing to which he credited the victory of his faith and life. I remember he sat and thought for a few minutes and then he opened his desk and pulled out a well-worn Bible and a book on the Christian vocation of a layman.

"Two things on my part," he said with a smile, "have made it possible for God to do the little he has done through me—my regular worship in church and this," and he pointed to the books and to his office. "Every morning for thirty years I have come into this place and I have spent in prayer at least thirty minutes before my secretary permits anyone to call or enter. First I wait in quiet thankfulness and adoration for a few moments. Then I read the Bible or a book like this until I find something that speaks to me in my condition. But the most important part of the time is when I pour out my heart before him and then wait in his presence. Always I find the day goes better and my direction is surer." And he quoted the words with which this meditation began:

> I keep the Lord always before me,
>   because he is at my right hand,
>   I shall not be moved.

Read the record of all spiritually alive persons and the same witness in one way or another will be given. "He who does not pray at some special time and some special place is not likely to pray at any time or any place." [8]

Fourteen years ago I too found the hit-and-miss habits of prayer utterly inadequate. My listening point had not been discovered and when I did try to pray it was more often than not to seek for a certain feeling to reassure me or to win God's approval for my own cherished plans. Once in awhile my prayers were genuine, but too often they were superficial or sadly lacking. One summer, after a near crack-up in the spring under the pressures of my ministry, I took off six weeks to study the lives of the saints. I came home with a new determination: the first thirty minutes or, if need be, the first hour in my study every morning would be spent in confronting God—not in preparation for a sermon—not in working on my problems—but in meeting God and learning to trust and listen. I would not be writing this today except that this habit has continued through these years. The time has not always produced a genuine experience of prayer and I have not always kept it; but when I have "set the Lord before me" in my conscious, thoughtful act of recollection, I too have been strong and serene.

Let me suggest four kinds of recollection which for me and countless persons in every age have been helpful:

Let us give him our waking thoughts. The first five minutes as I shave or make up my face—whichever the case may be—ask myself in his Presence, "Who am I?

Am I a little ego-centered, posing, scher[...] anxious self? Or am I the self you war[...] Lord? Free, confident, loving, trusting? No, [...] the first, but by your grace I am the other! I am capable of anything this day through you who give me the strength and wisdom I need!"

"Give him the first thoughts," said Henry Vaughan, "so shalt thou keep his companionship all the day and in him sleep."

Let us give him our growing thoughts. I set apart a time for reading, for devotional study, for quiet meditation. Fifteen, thirty, sixty minutes—some time regularly to read until I find God's word for me that day. Then I write it out in a spiritual notebook. If possible I will write out my response to this word by which God speaks to me. "This is what I have been doing. This is what I am going to do." A written confession and repentance, affirmation and decision, dedication and trust will help me to open the doors of my unconscious mind to the grace of God. I spend the last few minutes in quiet communion, letting the new affirmation or decision take hold of my innermost spirits. I pray for others, offer up my petition in the light of this new insight: this is giving God my growing thoughts.

Then let us give him our working thoughts. Of course it is necessary to do more than keep set times of prayer. There are times when an act of recollection can be made in a few seconds, but never except through a conscious determination to do it. It must never be done as a mere mental exercise, but always as an act of faith. A doctor recollects the Presence in between patients. A salesman

time he opens the door of his car. A secretary every
me she puts a new sheet of paper in the typewriter. A
housewife every time she answers the phone or the door
or climbs the stairs. As many times during the day as a
sense of fear, inadequacy, timidity, prejudice, or resentment comes, I decide again who I am in an uplifted
aspiration. Thus I give him my working thoughts.

Then let us give him our sleeping thoughts. Before I
go to sleep I look back over the day seeing where I have
failed, how often and when and why I acted out of the
false shell of my old self-image. I accept forgiveness with
a new surrender, forgive myself and others even as I am
forgiven, and with a new act of commitment and trust
go to sleep. Such thoughts have a remarkably purifying
influence on the twisted confusions of the subconscious.
They open the door to a new beginning as I awaken the
next morning to ask again, "Who am I? What shall I
do? And how shall I do it?"

Through it all God is waiting for my acceptance and
trust. I ask his beloved Son, my Lord, to teach me how to
meet him:

> Jesus, kneel beside me
>   In the dawn of day;
> Thine is prayer eternal—
>   Teach me how to pray!
>
> Master, work beside me
>   In the shining sun;
> Gently guide Thy servant
>   Till the work be done.

Saviour, watch beside me
In the closing light;
Lo, the evening cometh—
Watch with me this night!

Birds are winging homeward,
Sun and shadow cease;
Saviour, take my spirit
To Thy perfect peace.[9]
—ALLEN EASTMAN CROSS

4. I LEARN TO THINK IN THE PRESENCE OF GOD

"But what do I do in these times which I set apart to commune with God?" you are asking. "How do I recollect God and recognize his presence?"

There is no easy, simple answer. Sometimes one approach is better than others. May I suggest the three most often used: (a) the use of meditation or thinking in the presence of God; (b) the use of silence; and (c) letting the worship and fellowship of the Church, as the body of Christ, help us to realize communion with the Presence.

Most often in my own daily experience when the power of the worshiping community is not available, the practice of meditation has proved most helpful. I learn to think in the presence of God. That is I deliberately set certain thoughts in the center of my mind. I practice substitution: one thought displaces another and thus I arrive at the doorway of the temple of prayer where recollection, communion, silence before him are possible.

"Isn't that autosuggestion?" you ask. Indeed it is. I recall one of my most helpful teachers in the devotional life, Douglas V. Steere, answering this objection by asking, "All right, but which do you prefer, autosuggestion or heterosuggestion?" The simple truth is that there are only one of three ways in which a thought comes to our minds: (a) from outside—"hetero"—by radio, T.V., newspaper, and other sources of this nature; (b) from inside—"auto"—by consciously directed mind; or (c) from deeper inside—by my subconscious mind. What comes from the subconscious may indeed include suggestions from the Holy Spirit who dwells within us. But we may be so filled up with suggestions from outside that the Holy Spirit has little chance to speak.

Autosuggestion is in essence the place where the conscious mind and intelligent will begin to decide what happens in the deeper mind or unconscious heart rather than permitting our minds to be flooded and directed by everything that comes from the outside.

"The capacity to focus the attention on anything we choose is the greatest single evidence of our freedom," says William James. It has also the greatest potential for opening our minds to the Holy Spirit of God and his life-changing influences. Meditation is nothing more nor less than the discipline of my conscious mind by which I open the door for the Spirit of God.

In Taylor Caldwell's story, that which made coming into the little white room to sit and talk with the Man Who Listens so effective was just this: the attention was concentrated on one who heard and understood. Indeed this story is entirely true to life. For example, there was a brilliant young professor of electrical engineering in the University of Chicago whose name was H. B. Sharman. Agnostic, almost atheistic, he had no use for God or prayer or religion beyond the devotion to humanistic values. One day he heard almost by accident a minister in the chapel give a dare to the students: "If you claim to be scientific in your approach to life, how can you say there is nothing to Jesus' claims to be 'the way, and the truth, and the life' unless and until you have made the experiment of following him. I dare you to get acquainted with Jesus, his life and teachings, to discover what he said about the nature of God, of man and the universe, and to act upon it. Only then will you know whether or not it is true or false."

The young agnostic professor accepted the challenge and for months immersed his mind in the study of Jesus in the four gospels. As he set Jesus continually before him and committed himself to act on the faith Jesus lived, he began to pray. With prayer came a flood of new life. H. B. Sharman dedicated his time from then on to teaching other students the fine art of meditating on the life and teachings of Jesus. Through Y.M.C.A. sponsored seminars and camps in Canada and the United States, his method has been used by thousands of persons who though unable to know the human Jesus yet have become acquainted with the living Christ through meditating on his life, teachings, sacrificial death, and triumphant resurrection.[10]

Throughout the centuries the practice of meditating on the life and work of our Lord has been most fruitful in producing the listening point where real communion is possible. Francis of Sales in the sixteenth century; the Brothers of Common Life from which came *The Imitation of Christ* in the thirteenth and fourteenth centuries; Ignatius of Loyola founder of the Jesuits; and many others through the years, including present-day spiritual guides, have developed their own methods of meditating on the life of Jesus that have been helpful to thousands.

To illustrate: select a story in the life of Jesus such as the experience with the Samaritan woman at the well (John 4:4-26). Imagine you are this woman. Identify yourself with her problems and frustrations—her inability to get along with any husband so that she has had seven of them! (This might be especially helpful if you have been having conflicts in your own family lately!) You have heard of this wonderful teacher, but you have never met him. Now you look up as you draw water from the well and suddenly he is there. You try to picture him. You hear his request for a drink and your rebuke because he a Jew asked a drink of you a Samaritan woman. You hear his answer about the living water God gives and your skeptical retort. Then you are touched deeply by his words: "Everyone who drinks of this water will thirst again, but whoever drinks of the water that I shall give him will never thirst; the water that I shall give him will become in him a spring of water welling up to eternal life."

But you go on beyond the woman at that ancient well who said wistfully, "Sir, give me this water, that I may not thirst, nor come here to draw."

You ask him what he means by "living water" and

listen for his answer. You turn and read the sermon on the mount (Matt. 5-7) and seek to learn what he means by "asking and receiving," "How much more will your Father who is in heaven give good things to those who ask him." Or you read John 15, "If you abide in me, and my words abide in you, ask whatever you will." "What, Lord, do you mean by asking us to abide in you?"

Obviously such possibilities of meditation are endless. But take another example: Read Luke 15 in which Jesus describes what it means to be lost and found by the love of God. He tells the three parables of the lost coin, the lost sheep, and the lost son. Put yourself in place of these: In what way am I like the useless coin, the bewildered sheep, the rebellious son? Think on the character of God these stories reveal!

This method of visual imagination enables you to participate in experiences of long ago which now become contemporary: You are standing at the foot of the cross as Jesus cries, "Father, forgive them." You sense the tragedy and the suffering. "Here I stand, O Lord, to talk out all my bitterness and unforgiving hatred." And what a difference I feel as I speak my feelings in his presence.

This is the theme of *The Little World of Don Camillo.*[11] This is the story of a priest in a small village in Italy after World War II. He has a quick temper, and is so very human in his reactions to the unlovely attitudes of his parishioners and the other villagers, especially the Communists whom he hates. But every morning he comes into the church, stands before the crucifix, and spills all his foolish and even immoral desires. As he speaks his hot and hasty ideas and his enthusiasm for them begins to wane, his ideas seem less and less worthy, and before long he is kneeling in contrition and asking forgiveness. The One on the cross comes alive in his imagination, but back of the physical cross and the human imagination is the reality of the One who forever bears our sins and carries our sorrows!

If you are not able to visualize the Christ, choose some thought such as the words of Augustine, "Love God and do as you please." Through the spirit of Jesus' words and acts, meditate on what this means to you in your condition, this hour, this day.

Or use some incident in your life, some failure, some success, some humiliation. "What does this have to say to me of God's truth?" Think about your experience in the presence of God. There is all the difference between this and self-centered thinking which may lead to more and more frustration. *In the presence of God* you find insights into your sins as well as the symptoms that result and the power to conquer them one at a time.

There may be three steps to the recollection that leads to communion: (a) You begin rather cold. Prayer is difficult, but you concentrate your attention by willing to do so. (b) If you stay with it, something begins to happen as the Holy Spirit lights up the truth in your mind. This is what the saints call "infused recollection." (c) Sometimes—it may be rarely, but most of us have a few experiences of the kind—a burst of light comes. A sense of reality takes hold, "The witness of the Spirit with our spirits!" The truth catches fire and we *know*. Then with Browning's "*Abt Vogler*" after a period of meditation before the Lord we too cry, "The rest may reason and welcome; 'tis we musicians know." Put the words "We who wait before him" in place of the words "we musicians" and you have what he meant.

Ralph S. Cushman's words are a good example of the fine art of meditation by which the reality of God's forgiving love came to one man. Why not use this for your meditation, now?

Dear Christ, I think if only I could rest awhile
Down at thy knees, like John, and have thee smile
On me as I should lift my yearning face to thine,
And feel thy hand, in sweet embrace, placed warm in
    mine;
I think I could rise up again strong in thy strength divine,
If only I could feel thy hand on mine!

Sometimes I am so very weary, Lord;
Sometimes if I could only hear thy spoken word,
As Peter heard among the winds and waves of Galilee,
Even in sad rebuke, but know that thou are calling me;
I think I could do anything, go anywhere with thee,
If only I could hear thy voice calling me!

Forgive me, Lord, I hear; I hear! Forgive a child;
Forgive me, for the storms sometimes are wild;
Confused and beaten I forget how very near thou art;
Forgive me, for I will not ask to touch the fleshly part;
Only remind me once again how near thou art,
Christ of my heart! Christ of my heart! [12]

VIII. COMMUNION

1. PARTICIPATING IN THE CHURCH, THE BODY OF CHRIST, I ABIDE IN HIM AND HE IN ME

Reading what has gone before, some may mistakenly conclude that real Christian prayer is a vertical communion between my isolated soul and God. Nothing could be further from the truth. There is no communion with God in isolation, for God is a God of love who calls us to belong to his family. "He who says he loves God and does not love his brother is a liar." Thus we may summarize the emphasis of the writer of I John: "He who loves his brother abides in the light, and in it there is no cause for stumbling." (2:10.)

"Where two or three are gathered in my name, there am I in the midst of them." This promise of Jesus has been fulfilled in the experience of Christians in every age. Where two or three are gathered in worship and fellowship in the spirit of their Lord, there is the Church, "the body of Christ" as Paul describes it:

Now you are the body of Christ and individually members of it. . . . that through the church the manifold wisdom of God might now be made known . . . until we all attain to the unity of the faith and of the knowledge of the Son of

God, to mature manhood, to the measure of the stature of the fulness of Christ; . . . God who is rich in mercy, out of the great love with which he loved us, even when we were dead through our trespasses, made us alive together with Christ."

—I Cor. 12:27; Eph. 3:10; 4:13; 2:4-5

"God . . . made us alive *together* with Christ." We are not made alive separately. The twelve disciples were together with Christ in the physical presence of Jesus. Here it was easy to pray with him to the Heavenly Father who knew when even a sparrow fell and cared for each of them individually as a father cares for his sons. But when Jesus was crucified, dead, and buried they were thrown into confusion and despair. But on the first day of the week he appeared to them and they knew him. After the resurrection experiences they met in the Upper Room in a warm fellowship of remembrance in what they called the Eucharist (thanksgiving). When they broke the bread they found themselves bound together by his Spirit, as the two disciples in Emmaus had first witnessed "how he was known to them in the breaking of the bread." After all the questions are asked, the simple but elemental fact is: the experience of God in Christ never comes in isolation, but always in fellowship. What the physical presence of the human Jesus did for the twelve the fellowship of worshiping, serving believers did for them after the Resurrection and still does for us now.

God makes us alive *together* with Christ. We are not made alive separately. There is no real Christian prayer in isolation. D. L. Moody was talking one evening by the fireside with an old friend who said, "I believe in God, in prayer, but not in the church. I do not need the church." Moody said no word in answer, but with the tongs took a live coal from the fireplace and left it alone on the hearth until its warmth and beauty had disappeared and nothing was left but ashes. This was his answer. Without the fellowship, teaching, preaching, and worship of the church every one of us will burn out and die like that coal of fire.

There are really three kinds of prayer as Communion with God: (a) the prayer of worship with the great congregation, (b) the prayer of intimate fellowship in small groups, and (c) the prayer when we are alone physically, but never spiritually—for there is "the great cloud of witnesses" who have gone before and who come after. Even in this latter kind of personal prayer when we are physically alone, the church is there. We are either a part of the body of Christ then or we are separated from God. Sometimes of course illness or geographical distance makes physical participation in the body of Christ impossible; but the real presence of God is always found in communion with others.

If you find worship with the congregation of believers distasteful and even distracting, as some think it is, any one of three things is true: (a) either the particular congregation is completely bereft of the Spirit of Christ, which is very unlikely—surely two or three in it are in union with their Lord!—or (b) you have walls of stubborn hostility still between you and some of the people who worship there; or (c) you have not learned the meaning of humble, thankful worship.

Granted that some churches are more filled with the Spirit of Christ than others and some are more adapted to your needs than others, there surely is some church somewhere which may help you to find "the unity of the Spirit in the bond of peace."

"But," you ask, "how does the church help me to find real communion with God?" I answer, does not all our human experience declare that the faith of the several strengthens the faith of the one? The physical presence of Jesus, to whom God was real, ministered to the faith of the disciples. The physical presence of two or three, a dozen, a hundred, a thousand whose lives shine with the light of the glory of God ministers to me when I am struggling to believe. I am not talking of mass suggestion, though no doubt this has its part in church as well as a football game. I am speaking of shared witness which enables me to venture out in the darkness by faith and to find the Rock beneath.

> He bids us build each other up;
>   And, gathered into one,
> To our high calling's glorious hope,
>   We hand in hand go on.
>   —CHARLES WESLEY

For we are social beings, made for belonging. The sense of belonging to each other makes the sense of belonging to the family of God more real. "He is our peace, who has made us both one, and has broken down the dividing wall of hostility. . . . So then you are no longer strangers and sojourners, but you are . . . members of the household of God." (Eph. 2:14, 19.)

The belonging not only to a great congregation but to a small group is therefore most important if our communion with God is to be vital. We have seen in this age as in every age when Christianity has been powerful a renaissance of small groups.

Early Christians met in homes. Francis of Assisi began the awakening in the Middle Ages by the intimate fellowship of "the Little Brothers" as they called themselves. The Brothers of the Common Life in the fourteenth and fifteenth centuries made Christ alive to hundreds of thousands. The Wesleyan awakening in the eighteenth century would never have lasted but for the "class" and "band meetings." Frontier Christianity in America was vital through "experience meetings" and "prayer meetings." These gradually disappeared in most churches because they became too rigid and stereotyped, too often used for display. Today we have a rebirth of small groups meeting together for vital Christian fellowship. Some are called "prayer cells." Others, "churches in the home." They are being formed by persons who know the need of an intimate fellowship group in which they may share their experiences and problems and find a deeper reality in their prayers.[1]

How priceless indeed is the experience described in the hymn:

> All praise to our redeeming Lord,
> Who joins us by His grace,
> And bids us, each to each restored,

Together seek His face.

. . . .

We all partake the joy of one;
The common peace we feel:
A peace to worldly minds unknown,
A joy unspeakable.
—CHARLES WESLEY

Such fellowship in the body of Christ does three things: (a) It removes the hindrances to prayer in our loneliness and isolation as "each to each" is restored. (b) Shared joys are always deeper and fuller. All of us have had something of worth happen to us and our first impulse was to say, "If I could just tell someone who could rejoice with me!" (c) We "build each other up" in the grace of God—not egoistic backslapping. The church is no mutual admiration society—for the exaltation of egos—but a fellowship of strugglers who are learning to believe together.

Love found me in the wilderness, at cost
Of painful quest, when I myself had lost.

Love on its shoulders joyfully did lay
Me, weary with the greatness of my way.[2]
—RICHARD C. TRENCH

This is the church! How irreplaceable is the inspiration and help of the church when with humility and faith I let its worship and fellowship become the body of Christ in which I find the real presence of God more surely than any other place! Then I am able to go out into the world and share the love and truth of Christ as a peacemaker, helping to break down the walls of hostilities that divide us as families, races, and nations. "For in him all things hold together. He is the head of the body, the Church; . . . For he is our peace, who has made us both one." (Col. 1:17-18; Eph. 2:14.)

Dear Lord, who holds us all as one
    Beneath Thy kindly gaze,
Through growth and joy, through storm and sun,
When patience ends and love seems done,
    Forgive our separate ways.

O Thou in whom God chose to dwell,
    Join us in Christlike peace,
May we Thy tender kindness tell,
As Thou dost each one's fear dispel,
    So grant to each release.

May we forgive as we're forgiven,
    Forbear in Christian love,
Receive this best foretaste of heaven,
Thy precious power so freely given,
    To rise with Thee above.

Dear Lord, endow each word and thought
    With Thy great truth, that we
May in our hearts be fully brought
To know the greatness Thou hast wrought.
    O make us one in Thee! [3]

2. "STILL, STILL WITH THEE"

The most real and precious part of my prayer and yours as a Christian is far beyond the asking stage or even the confessing and forgiving stage: It is prayer of communion with the Presence. Such exalted prayer was known to a few of the great spirits even before Christ. The Books of Psalms and of the Prophets in the Old Testament are filled with beautiful testimonies such as these:

> By day the Lord commands his
>   steadfast love;
>   and at night his song is with me,
>   a prayer to the God of my life.
> —Ps. 42:8

> For God alone my soul waits
>   in silence;
>   From him comes my salvation.
> He only is my rock and my salva-
>   tion,
>   my fortress; I shall not be greatly
>   moved.
> —Ps. 62:1-2

> When my soul was embittered,
>   when I was pricked in heart,
> I was stupid and ignorant,
>   I was like a beast toward thee.
> Nevertheless I am continually with
>   thee;
>   thou dost hold my right hand.
> Thou dost guide me with thy
>   counsel,
>   and afterward thou wilt receive
>   me to glory.
> Whom have I in heaven but thee?

And there is nothing upon earth
   that I desire beside thee.
My flesh and my heart may fail,
   but God is . . . my portion forever.

.   .   .   .

But for me it is good to be near
   God.
                          —Ps. 73:21-26, 28

When I awake, I shall be satisfied
   with beholding thy form.
                          —Ps. 17:15

When I awake, I am still with
   thee.
                          —Ps. 139:18

The sense of the Presence described so poignantly in the Old Testament psalms is brought even to sharper focus in the experience through the living Christ of the Holy Spirit as described in the New Testament. According to John 14:16-18, Jesus promised his disciples:

I will pray the Father, and he will give you another Counselor, to be with you for ever, even the Spirit of truth, whom the world cannot receive, because it neither sees him nor knows him; you know him, for he dwells with you, and will be in you. "I will not leave you desolate; I will come to you."

Read the New Testament to see his promise remarkably fulfilled. Read the life of every vital Christian since and the reality of the Presence is the one most common experience: from Paul to Polycarp, from Augustine to Luther, from Francis of Assisi to Wesley, from Rufus Jones to the ordinary Christian today. "The life of prayer," said Teresa of Avila, "is just a love of God and a liking to be with him."

Indeed the prayer of a trusting soul is so very simple we are likely to miss it in looking for something more complex. It is like quietly opening a door and slipping into the very presence of God. It is waiting in the silence to the still small voice:

> Perhaps to petition
> Or only to listen,
> It matters not,
> Just to be there
> In his presence
> Is prayer.
>   —ANONYMOUS

When communion with the Presence is real, as with old friends, we don't need to talk, much less ask for something—though when we are in need we always ask —but we commune together. In the prayer of confession we let go. In the prayer of silence he quiets the storms. We have lifted our hearts in adoration to the One whose majestic greatness and love is indescribable. Now we wait and are changed in his presence. "Our minds . . . bubble and heave . . . like a fermenting morass," says Gerald Heard; and out of the experience comes a change of being as we accept ourselves as we are and can be in the loving reality of God's presence.

Then as was described in the preceding chapter, I have

what some have called "infused contemplation" in which I cease to act or think as an isolated, self-centered individual but I am "carried forward" as if by "an inflowing stream of light" into

> . . . that blessed mood,
> In which the burthen of the mystery,
> In which the heavy and weary weight
> Of all this unintelligible world,
> Is lightened—that serene and blessed mood
> In which the affections gently lead us on—
>
> . . . .
>
> While with an eye made quiet by the power
> Of harmony, and the deep power of joy
> We see into the life of things.[4]
> —WILLIAM WORDSWORTH

There are all stages in this kind of communion. Some have more and some have less feeling. Others have only a quiet sense of belonging. But of one thing I am sure: "For me it is good to be near God!"

Often his presence is ministered to us in the natural world about us. As I write this, one of the tallest persons spiritually, I know, has just left my study in the pines of Vermont. He was a barber in a little Vermont town for fifty years until he retired. His age is eighty-two but his spirit is young as the rainbow. He was telling me how he missed being able to go fishing in the clear brooks of his native mountains as he once used to do.

"Many's the time as I walked under the arched cathedral of the woods and cast my line in the sparkling water that rushed joyfully down the mountain, I stopped to kneel and pray—just to thank God for all his gifts of beauty and love. God always is near to me when I am in these lovely places."

But I knew he also met God regularly in the communion of the church where he never missed a service of worship.

For him and for all of us who find the communion with God in nature, the trees and the mountains, the water and the flowers are translucent through the Spirit of Christ, without which indeed nature may be more terrifying than blessed. For example, consider the way Anna Bunston de Bary's "Under a Wiltshire Apple Tree" finds a garden sacramental of her Lord:

> . . . when I do see
> Thik apple tree
> An' stoopin' limb
> All spread wi' moss,
> I think of Him
> And how He talk wi' me.

> . . . .

> He never pushed the garden door,
> He left no footmark on the floor;
> I never heard 'Un stir nor tread
> And yet His Hand do bless my head,
> And when 'tis time for work to start
> I takes Him with me in my heart.

> And when I die, pray God I see
> At very last thik apple tree
> An' stoopin' limb,

> And think of Him,
> And all He been to me.[5]

If experiences such as these are illusions, they have done more good, brought more cheer, added more strength and hope to life than all the so-called "practical" experiences. Since some of us believe they are real, these experiences with the Presence should be the object of our deepest quest—the greatest gift for which we should ask God to make us fit to receive. After all what an amazing, incredible thing that I, an infinitely small part of this mighty universe, should be made to share in the communion with my Creator-Father-Friend!

"Mystical!" you say. Of course! But remember, there is a healthy and unhealthy mysticism. Like all other human experiences it may be misused and prostituted, but in one way or another it is the heart of all great religion: "The personal conviction by an individual that the human spirit and the divine Spirit have met, have found each other and are in mutual reciprocal correspondence as spirit with Spirit." [6]

As Christians, Quakers and Methodists, Roman Catholics and Baptists, we all find our religion vital when there is "an immediate awareness of relation with God, an intimate consciousness of the divine Presence. It is religion in its most acute, intense and living stage." [7]

The attempt to practice the Presence may be ruined in one of three ways: (a) we may seek an experience for the experience's sake and lose God while seeking for some predefined proof of his presence; (b) we may identify the presence of God with a mood, an emotion, or a feeling and thereby lose him; and (c) most destructive of all we may use this experience as a proof of our superiority over others. Read Paul's first letter to the Corinthians, chapters twelve, thirteen, and fourteen, to see his warning against these dangers: "If I speak in the [ecstatic] tongues of men and of angels, but have not love, I am a noisy gong and a clanging cymbal. . . . Love is not jealous or boastful; it is not arrogant or rude . . . it is not irritable or resentful."

He admits that he has had experiences that approach the state of ecstasy; but "I will show you a still more excellent way," and he goes on to write this beautiful hymn to love, part of which is quoted above. Yes, "any one who does not have the Spirit of Christ does not belong to him." (Rom. 8:9.)

True communion with the Presence is a healthy and life-giving relationship in which we seek God—not an experience, not an emotion, a mood, or a feeling—in which we renounce any test of ecstasy or illumination as evidence. What then is the evidence that we have been with him? "The fruit of the Spirit is love, joy, peace, patience, kindness, goodness, faithfulness, gentleness, self-control!" (Gal. 5:22.) The encounter by faith with the Spirit brings us not only illumination in darkness, guidance in difficult times, strength and courage for the "weary, plodding miles," but also "a certainty in the probings which have shamed and the purgations which have cleansed and the promptings which have demanded action." [8] These experiences of communion are self-authenticating in the certainty that this is the way life is meant to be. This is that for which we are made. This is indeed "the foretaste of heaven."

Yes, this communion with the Presence in which all life has meaning is veritably to live in the kingdom of heaven now! And "it does not yet appear what we shall be, but we know that when he appears we shall be like him, for we shall see him as he is!" (I John 3:2.)

Still, still with thee, when purple morning breaketh,
    When the birds waketh and the shadows flee;
Fairer than morning, lovelier than daylight,
    Dawns the sweet consciousness, I am with thee.

. . . .

So shall it be at last, in that bright morning,
    When the soul waketh, and life's shadows flee:
In that hour, fairer than daylight dawning,
    Shall rise the glorious thought, I am with thee.
               —Harriet Beecher Stowe

NOTES

I. ADORATION

[1] "The Little Gate to God" ("The Postern Gate") from *Walter Rauschenbusch* by Dores Robinson Sharpe. Copyright © 1942, by The Macmillan Company. Used by permission of Carl Rauschenbusch.

[2] Quoted by Albert D. Belden, *The Practice of Prayer* (New York: Harper & Brothers, 1954).

[3] F. E. Christmas (ed.) *Hear My Prayer* (London: Hodder & Stoughton, Ltd., n. d.), pp. 466-67.

[4] Rauschenbusch, *op. cit.*

[5] *Ibid.*

[6] *Mysticism and Logic* (London: G. Allen Unwin Co., 1951), pp. 47-48.

[7] "That We May Sing," from *The Greatest of These . . .* by Jane Merchant. Copyright 1954 by Pierce & Washabaugh. By permission of Abingdon Press.

[8] "The Lord Is My Light."

[9] Thomas R. Kelly, *A Testament of Devotion* (New York: Harper & Brothers, 1941). Used by permission of Harper & Row, Publisher. P. 65.

[10] C. F. Andrews, *Christ and Prayer* (New York: Harper & Brothers, 1937). Used by permission of Hodder & Stoughton Limited and Harper & Row, Publisher. Pp. 66, 67, 68, 69.

[11] Quoted by Douglas V. Steere, *On Beginning from Within* (New York: Harper & Brothers, 1943), p. 79.

[12] *Four Quartets* (New York: Harcourt, Brace & Company, 1943). Used by permission of Harcourt, Brace & World, Inc. and Faber and Faber Ltd. P. 15.

II. CONFESSION

[1] "To a Louse."

[2] Thomas a Kempis, *The Imitation of Christ.*

[3] Quoted by Friedrich Heiler.

[4] Helmut Gollwitzer et al. (eds.), *Dying We Live; the Final Messages and Records of the Resistance* (New York: Pantheon Books, Inc., 1956), p. 135.

[5] Charles F. Whiston (ed.), François Fénelon's *Christian Perfection* (New York: Harper & Brothers, 1947). Used by permission of Harper & Row, Publisher. Pp. 124-25.

[6] From *The Poems of St. John of the Cross, Original Spanish Texts,* and New English Versions by John Frederick Nims. Published by Grove Press, Inc. Copyright © 1959 by John Frederick Nims. P. 31.

[7] "Abt Vogler."

[8] Raymond Bernard Blakney, *Meister Eckhart, A Modern Translation* (New York: Harper & Brothers, 1957). Used by permission of Harper & Row, Publisher. Pp. 126, 127.

[9] Attributed to Bishop Leofric, eleventh century.

[10] *Brother Lawrence*, Trans. from the French (New York: Fleming H. Revell Company, 1895), pp. 24, 25-26.

[11] *Ibid.,* p. 26.

[12] *Ibid.,* p. 19.

III. COMMITMENT

[1] Thomas a Kempis, *The Imitation of Christ* (Philadelphia: Henry Altemus, 1894), p. 135.

[2] "Prayer." *Poems with Power.*

[3] Mendelssohn, *Elijah.*

[4] "Whoso Draws Nigh to God."

[5] David Head, *He Sent Leanness; A Book of Prayers for the Natural Man.* Reprinted with permission of The Macmillan Company and Epworth Press. P. 23.

[6] "Follow me" by John Oxenham. Used by permission of Miss Theo Oxenham.

[7] "The Wreck of the Deutschland." From *Poems of Gerard Manley Hopkins,* third edition, edited by W. H. Gardner. Copyright 1948 by Oxford University Press, Inc. Reprinted by permission.

[8] Prayer of Ignatius Loyola.

IV. PETITION

[1] Paul I. Wellman, *The Chain* (Garden City, New York: Doubleday & Company, Inc., 1949), p. 144.

[2] "Thy sea, O God, so great." Copyright 1926 Christian Century Foundation. Reprinted by permission from *The Christian Century* and Winfred E. Garrison.

[3] *Alcoholic Anonymous* (New York: Works Publishing Co., 1939), p. 71.

[4] From *It's Good to Be Alive* by Roy Campanella. Copyright © 1959 by Roy Campanella. Used by permission of Little, Brown & Co. Pp. 204-6.

[5] "The preceding five verses are from "The Quest" by Chester B.

Emerson. Used by permission of Chester B. Emerson.

⁶ Gollwitzer, op. cit., pp. xx.

⁷ "Prayer for a Time of Turmoil" from *The Glory of God* by Georgia Harkness. Copyright 1943 by Whitmore & Stone. By permission of Abingdon Press.

⁸ "The One Thing" from *Think About These Things* by Jane Merchant. Copyright © 1956 by Pierce & Washabaugh. By permission of Abingdon Press.

⁹ "Prayer for the New Year."

¹⁰ Paraphrase of François Fénelon's prayer in *Christian Perfection*, op. cit., p. 125.

V. INTERCESSION

¹ John Donne, *Devotions*, XVII.

² See also Eph. 1:16; 6:18. Phil. 4:6, 12. Thess. 1:2. Phil. 4.

³ *A Serious Call to a Devout and Holy Life* (Philadelphia: The Westminster Press, 1948), p. 308.

⁴ Richard Trench.

⁵ "Prayer" from *Idylls of the King*.

⁶ *The Religious Consciousness* (New York: The Macmillan Company, 1920).

⁷ *That Immortal Sea* (Nashville: Abingdon Press, 1954), p. 132.

⁸ "Fra Lippo Lippi."

⁹ Alexander Whyte, *Thomas Shepard, Pilgrim Father and Founder of Harvard* (1909), pp. 73-74.

¹⁰ From *The Book of Offices*. Used by permission of The Epworth Press.

¹¹ From *I Will Lift Up Mine Eyes* by Glenn Clark. Used by permission of Harper & Brothers. P. 49.

VI. TRUST

¹ "The Place of Peace." Used by permission of Virgil Markham.

² Smiley Blanton and Norman Vincent Peale, *Faith Is the Answer* (New York and Nashville: Abingdon-Cokesbury Press, 1940), pp. 27-28.

³ Daniel A. Poling, *Faith Is Power for You* (New York: Greenberg, Publisher, 1950), pp. 29, 30.

⁴ From *Complete Poems of Robert Frost*. Copyright 1942 by Robert Frost. Reprinted by permission of Holt, Rinehart and Winston, Inc. and *The New York Times*.

⁵ James Martineau.

⁶ François Fénelon, "Teach Me."

VII. RECOLLECTION

¹ (New York: Alfred A. Knopf, Inc., 1958), p. 9.

² (New York: William Collins Sons & Co., Ltd., 1961).

³ *Ibid.*, pp. 325-26.

[4] Kelley, *Ibid.*, p. 38.

[5] C. S. Lewis, *The Screwtape Letters* (New York: The Macmillan Company, 1943), p. 29.

[6] Abbé de Tourville, *Letters of Direction* (London: Dacre Press, 1949). Used by permission of A. & C. Black Ltd. and Thomas Y. Crowell Company.

[7] Quoted by Robert I. Gannon, "Words to Remember." Reprinted from *This Week Magazine*. Copyrighted 1949 by the United Newspapers Magazine Corporation.

[8] Theodore Roosevelt.

[9] Used by permission of Mrs. Robert P. Bingham.

[10] H. B. Sharman, *Jesus in the Records* (New York: Association Press, 1939) and *The Records of Jesus* (New York: Harper & Brothers, 1917).

[11] Giovanni Guareschi (New York: Pellegrini and Cudahy, 1950).

[12] "Christ of My Heart," from *Spiritual Hilltops*, copyright renewal 1960 by Ralph S. Cushman. By permission of Abingdon Press.

VIII. COMMUNION

[1] c.f. John L. Casteele, *Spiritual Renewal Through Personal Groups* (New York: Association Press, 1957) and Harold W. Freer and Frances B. Hall, *Two or Three Together* (New York: Harper & Brothers, 1954).

[2] "Love Found Me."

[3] A prayer hymn for unity in Christ written especially by me for Christian Family Week. Tune "Elton Rest."

[4] "Lines Composed a Few Miles Above Tintern Abbey."

[5] From *Collected Poems of Anna Bunston de Bray*, published by Mitre Press, London.

[6] Elizabeth Janet Gray, *Friend of Life; the Biography of Rufus M. Jones* (Philadelphia: J. B. Lippincott Company, 1958), p. 251.

[7] *Ibid.*, p. 251.

[8] Albert Edward Day, *Autobiography of Prayer* (New York: Harper & Brothers, 1952), p. 51.

Study Guide

Delia Halverson

INTRODUCTION

We find many opportunities to pray. We pray within a group; we pray in unison with a group; we pray privately. The personal prayer is unique. It is just that—personal. It works toward a relationship. Through personal prayer a relationship matures between the person and God. Bishop Lance Webb's book *The Art of Personal Prayer* helps guide development of that relationship.

Any study is of little use unless it becomes part of the student's life. A spiritual prayer notebook helps one's study to become part of the individual. Thoughts, ideas, and suggestions entered in the notebook during study not only stimulate deeper thoughts but also offer opportunities for reflection as study progresses.

As a group using this study, designate in advance a leader for each session. The leader encourages everyone to share in the discussion and aids the group in keeping the primary point of discussion along the study theme.

Prayer will naturally be a part of each individual's study time as well as part of the group time. The group may decide to set aside a certain time each day to pray for one another's growth. Some groups find that the period between 7:00 and 8:00 A.M. is routine enough for each member to select a time to pray, perhaps while dressing or during breakfast.

At the beginning of each session the leader may stimulate interest by offering opportunity for participants to share something meaningful from their preparation. Using the thoughts that are shared, the leader may use them as a springboard to one of the discussion questions, thus allowing the discussion to rise naturally from the group. During the discussion the leader should feel free to move to various questions in the guide when the group response leads in that direction. The order of discussion is not so important as the natural response of the group.

I. ADORATION

Matthew 6:9-13
- The second line of the Lord's Prayer is "hallowed be thy name." What do we mean when we pray those words?
- List reasons you adore God:
    I adore God because he gave me a lovely family.
    I adore God because he created springtime.
    I adore God because _____
    Now, cross out everything after the first three words of each sentence.
- How does adoration differ from seeking peace and reflecting within ourselves?
- How can adoration change our lives?

- Discuss Bishop Webb's two types of perspective from which we may look at life:
    —When we feel we are insignificant particles of a mass of universe, but powerless beyond ourselves, of what use is adoration?
    —How does this change when we view ourselves as created, yet a part of our Creator today?
    —More particularly, how does the Christian viewpoint of God encourage and increase adoration of him?
- Discuss times when we are most likely to push God for a solution to our problem before first releasing our adoration for him.
- What are some of the "other priceless expressions" of Christian prayer when adoration precedes all else in our praying?
- How can we prepare to communicate with God—to hear his approach to us? His approaches are invariably expressions of his attributes—such as his love; his presence; his spirit; which give courage, strength, and hope.

II. CONFESSION

Psalm 139:23-24
- Have someone read aloud to the group the second paragraph, page 26, of the study book. Then focus on the major ideas in it:
    —The effects of the prayer of confession.
    —The place of truth about ourselves in our praying.
    —Obtaining power for freedom to live the truth.
- What part does faith play in our prayer of confession? What part does God's love play?
- What is the meaning of the phrase "in Christ"? What

bearing does being in Christ have in our prayer of confession?

- Discuss the nature of the shell of the "false universe" surrounding us.
- What sort of false ego do we build about ourselves to prove we are important?
- Something to remember: "The real truth about me is far more wonderful than this false ego I am trying to buttress and make secure" (p. 27).
- Review the three suggestions for discovering the self-idols that keep us separated from God and life. (See pp. 35-36.)
- Discuss the difference between symptoms of sins and sins themselves.
  —List several sins and symptoms stemming from those sins.
  —Should we pray about the sins or the symptoms?
- Psychology and psychiatry are important in analysis of human behavior and problems which afflict mind and spirit.
  —Consider at what point the prayer of faith goes beyond psychology.
  —How can the light of God in Christ lead us to rejection of our false ego and false exterior and open our hearts to the divine light given us in Christ?
- Freedom in prayer is not something easily obtained. Focus on the four ways suggested by Bishop Webb. (See p. 43.) Reading these aloud in the group may stimulate helpful comment.
- Self-will can stop us short in our prayer of confession. How is this so?
- How do we achieve honest confession of our sins?
- Describe the one perfection possible for us on earth.

—Is it a longing only, or a satisfying achievement?

—A worthy intention, or a desire never perfectly realized?

—A fact, or a dream worthy of lifelong pursuit?

- What does the Collect for Purity say to us today? Rewrite it in everyday words, in today's language. (See p. 40.)

III. COMMITMENT

2 Corinthians 4:7-14

- Make a list of things most important to you.
  - —Cross off things you could live without in an emergency.
  - —Cross off things you could do without should utter chaos come and your life itself be threatened.
  - —What is left is your subconscious prayer, that to which you are committed.
- How do we know when we have answered "no" to God's plan for the physical world? How do we know when we have answered "no" to God's plan for our personal and social universe?
- How do we sometimes limit our commitment to God? How can we liken praying to swimming?
- Can we pray wholeheartedly? What is the difference between a halfhearted search for God and a wholehearted one? (Refer to second complete paragraph on page 52 for help in answering.)
- Under what condition is our praying contradictory?
- Of what use is the practice of "saying prayers," form prayers, for private use? For group use?
- "I can do all things in him who strengthens me." (Philippians 4:13, RSV) Which words are most important in this verse: "I" or "in him"? Why?

IV. PETITION

John 15:1-8

- What is the difference between prayer and magic?
- In what ways does persistence in prayer help us?
- Is prayer a natural law? If so, in what sense? If not, what is a rational attitude as we pray regarding things subject to "natural law"?
- Share a time when you were so persistent in your prayer petitions to God that you were not open to hear the answer.
- Share times when a door you prayed would open remained closed, but when you turned the matter over to God's will in your life better opportunities to do his will opened up for you.
- Outline a petition prayer.
  —How do we ask in the wrong way?
  —How can we change a self-centered prayer to a God-centered one and still ask for our needs?
  —How should we end our prayer of petition?
- What is the real test of your prayer—the answer or the spirit in which you pray? What is the relation of the spirit in which we pray to the answer God gives?
- What are some of the attitudes of heart and mind needful in praying the petition prayer?

V. INTERCESSION

Philemon 6–7

- When did you pray with someone? How did you feel? Uneasy? Self-conscious?
- Why ought we to pray for others—from our viewpoint? From God's viewpoint?

- Have you ever given up on prayer? What was your belief in prayer at the time?
- How does intercessory prayer differ from mental telepathy?
- Discuss similarities between prayer and a scientist discovering the force of electricity.
- How is our prayer related to God's limit he places on himself?
- How can your praying or not praying make a difference in your influence on others? In what other ways does our praying help others?
- How can your praying for others help you also?
- Discuss the three steps in praying for others suggested by Bishop Webb. (See pp. 97-98.)
- With someone specific in mind, write a prayer of intercession in that person's behalf. Begin with adoration of God and then move on through the "three steps" suggested. Do not hurry in the writing. Give yourself time to make the suggested preparations and commitments before proceeding with the writing of each portion of your prayer.

VI. TRUST

1 John 3:19-24
- Discuss what effect our belief in God's will over the universe has on our trust in him.
- How does a prayer of trust remove fear?
- What three things are the heart of praying well?
- What is the kingdom of God?
- What makes us part of the kingdom of God?
- What is the meaning of Rufus Jones's phrase, the "Double Search"?

- Relate situations when you failed to trust God's solution to your problems and branched out on your own.
- How does this affect our prayer relationship with God?
- How can our prayers of adoration prepare us for the trust necessary in prayer? Can we have one without the other?

VII. RECOLLECTION

Luke 10:38-42
- Read the account of Jesus' conversation with the woman at the well in Samaria (John 4:4-26).
  - —What things might she have needed to relate to Christ?
  - —How might she have felt when suddenly she found herself in the presence of the Messiah?
- When have you needed to talk to someone about something but found no one to listen. If you wish, tell what it was about.
- Define *recollection* in the sense in which Bishop Webb uses it. (See pp. 124-128.)
- Consider times when you let the pressures of everyday life push aside your need to relate things to God, to communicate with him through prayer.
- What is a "listening point" and how does it relate to one's prayer life?
- How can we set up a practice of recalling God frequently in our everyday life? Suggest routine actions we may select as triggers to express adoration of God. Share with the group "listening points" (both place and time) you have developed. How do they fit into your life routine?

- How important is your prayer in times of ease as compared to your prayer in times of pressure?
- Can we call on God as naturally, as trustingly, as unashamedly, during a crisis if that is the only time we speak to him? Why?
- Discuss ways you can practice the four kinds of recollection Bishop Webb suggests (waking thoughts, growing thoughts, working thoughts, sleeping thoughts).
- Think of ways and means to recollect God and to recognize his presence. Give attention to the suggestions found in Section 4 of this Chapter VII. Consider especially such details as
    —learning to think in God's presence
    —thought substitution
    —ways thought comes to us
    —place and function of autosuggestion as related to conscious mind, intelligent will, and the deeper mind (unconscious heart).
- Discuss the meaning of "meditation."
    —Is its purpose to generate self-centered thinking?
    —What place should Christ hold in our meditation?
    —As we meditate, can our experiences say anything to us about God's truth?
    —Where does meditation put us in relation to God's presence? What rewarding perspective does meditation provide? What insight into our sins and their symptoms? What influx of power to conquer them one by one?
- Recollection (waiting before God) puts us on the road to communion with him.
    —What are three possible steps we may experience in moving from recollection to communion?
    —Describe the nature of each step.

—Does your prayer experience, your meditation, your recollection, confirm these steps?

—Which step is most difficult to experience?

VIII. COMMUNION

Ephesians 4:1-6

- What is the ultimate purpose of the church? Read aloud the paragraph beginning at the bottom of page 147. Is it a good working statement of the ultimate purpose of the church?
- Jesus was human. To experience God through Jesus we need other people. How do other people we know today affect our lives when we worship together?
- How do Christians of the past help us when we worship as a Christian group?
- Share with the group the story of a person whose great faith has been an inspiration to you. If possible, would a worship experience shared with that person be more meaningful to you? Explain.
- What are three things that fellowship in the body of Christ does for the members? (See p. 147.)
- Discuss examples of times you have ruined opportunities to practice the Presence by the ways Bishop Webb mentions:
   —seeking experience for experience's sake,
   —seeking a mood or feeling,
   —using the experience as an ego trip.
- How has your prayer life changed with the study of this book?
- What changes do you think you can yet make to improve your prayer life?